SCOTNOTES
Number 37

Scottish War Poetry 1914–1945

David Goldie and
Roderick Watson

Association for Scottish Literary Studies 2017

Published by
Association for Scottish Literary Studies
Scottish Literature
7 University Gardens
University of Glasgow
Glasgow G12 8QH
www.asls.org.uk

ASLS is a registered charity no. SC006535

First published 2017

Text © David Goldie and Roderick Watson

All rights reserved. No part of this book may be
reproduced, stored in a retrieval system, or
transmitted in any form or means, electronic,
mechanical, photocopying, recording or otherwise,
without the prior permission of the
Association for Scottish Literary Studies.

A CIP catalogue for this title
is available from the British Library

ISBN 978-1-906841-31-7

CONTENTS

	Page
Introduction	1
The First World War: 1914–1918	11
The Pattern of Expectation	11
The Anticipation of War	17
Poetry Goes to War	25
The War with Form	31
Language	39
The Home Front	43
Memory	49
The Second World War: 1939–1945	57
'This war, like the next war ...'	57
Total War	61
The Home Front	63
The Burning World	72
Remembering	93
Notes	99
Select Bibliography	101
Further Reading	103

SCOTNOTES

Study guides to major Scottish writers and literary texts

Produced by the Education Committee
of the Association for Scottish Literary Studies

Series Editors
Lorna Borrowman Smith
Ronald Renton

Editorial Board
Ronald Renton
(Convener, Education Committee, ASLS)
Craig Aitchison
Diane Anderson
Gillin Anderson
Laurence Cavanagh
Professor John Corbett
Dr Emma Dymock
Dr Maureen Farrell
Dr Morna Fleming
Professor Douglas Gifford
Simon Hall
Jean Hillhouse
John Hodgart
Bob Hume
Katrina Lucas
Catrina McGillivray
Ann MacKinnon
Dr David Manderson
Professor Alan Riach
Dr Gillian Sargent
Lorna Borrowman Smith

THE ASSOCIATION FOR SCOTTISH LITERARY STUDIES
aims to promote the study, teaching and writing of Scottish literature, and to further the study of the languages of Scotland.

To these ends, the ASLS publishes works of Scottish literature; literary criticism and in-depth reviews of Scottish books in *Scottish Literary Review*; and scholarly studies of language in *Scottish Language*. It also publishes *New Writing Scotland*, an annual anthology of new poetry, drama and short fiction, in Scots, English and Gaelic. ASLS has also prepared a range of teaching materials covering Scottish language and literature for use in schools.

All the above publications are available as a single 'package', in return for an annual subscription. Enquiries should be sent to:

ASLS
Scottish Literature
7 University Gardens
University of Glasgow
Glasgow G12 8QH

Tel/fax +44 (0)141 330 5309
e-mail **office@asls.org.uk**
or visit our website at **www.asls.org.uk**

All the Scottish war poems referred to in this Scotnote can be found in the anthology *From the Line: Scottish War Poetry 1914–1945*, edited by David Goldie and Roderick Watson (Glasgow: ASLS, 2014). The page references given in brackets in the text refer to this volume.

INTRODUCTION

The English poets of the First World War are justly celebrated for the powerful and compassionate account they have given us of what modern war is really like. The poems of Wilfred Owen and Siegfried Sassoon in particular have come to define what we think of as 'war poetry', and for many people their historical understanding of the 1914–18 conflict has been largely shaped by these writers. There were, however, many more poets of the time whose voices are equally powerful, if not quite so well remembered today. A significant proportion of them were Scottish, just as a significant proportion of the British army, and of the casualties suffered during both wars, were men from Scottish regiments. Roderick Watson Kerr, who survived the war, and Charles Hamilton Sorley, who was killed by a sniper at the Battle of Loos in 1915, have been widely recognised as among the best poets of the Great War, as have others, from John Buchan and Joseph Lee to Violet Jacob and Mary Symon. What is less well known, perhaps, is the major contribution made by Scottish writers to the very best poetry of the Second World War. Poets such as Hamish Henderson, Naomi Mitchison, G. S. Fraser, George Campbell Hay and Sorley MacLean were all caught up in the global conflict that was 1939–1945, and their poetry is an unforgettable response to the tensions of those years. This study seeks to do justice to all these Scottish poets and to the times they endured during the two greatest conflicts of the twentieth century.

*

It used to be a commonplace, in post-war families, to remember that father, or grandpa, 'never spoke about the war'. From what we know about post traumatic stress disorder today, we can only guess at the distress that was endured in silence by a significant percentage of the men who returned from combat in 1919 and 1945. Others were more fortunate, and hundreds of ordinary men and women, with no artistic pretensions, were motivated to write their own accounts of what they had seen and what it meant to them. Wilfred Owen did this, writing some of his most famous poems as an act of convalescence, encouraged by his doctor and by Siegfried Sassoon who was a fellow patient at Craiglockhart Hospital in Edinburgh. The Scottish poet J. B. Salmond was also a patient at Craiglockhart, and took over the editorship of its house magazine, the *Hydra*, from Owen, helping others discover the therapeutic benefits of writing prose and poetry.

There was also trauma and a need to speak among those who took part in their own personal conflicts well away from the battlefields: the civilians who took no part in the fighting but who suffered the fears and uncertainties that might follow defeat; those who worked in support of the war, making munitions, growing food, caring for the wounded, keeping families together in a time of crisis; and those many mothers and fathers, wives, and children who suffered shattering, life-altering bereavement. These too sought in words, whether written by themselves or by others, forms of expression that might make them feel less helpless and disempowered, or words of consolation that might take the bitter edge from their grief.

Such writing from direct experience, done by ordinary people as a matter of personal record, or personal therapy, or as political protest, is never to be underestimated. The writers in this study, however, were determined to be poets from the start, and the stories they bring us have the authenticity of individual experience still further enhanced by their developing craft. Such experience is not easily expressed, nor easily forgotten.

Some, especially in the first war, found themselves struggling against the very forms they had inherited: trying to express the unfamiliar, sometimes horrific experiences of technological and total war by way of the often genteel and euphemistic conventions they had inherited from their Victorian and Edwardian predecessors. Roderick Watson Kerr, in his poem 'June 1918' (31), found himself having to compound in one poem two wholly antagonistic approaches to the same subject: the first stanza taking the form of a consoling seasonal poem maintaining a Romantic faith in nature, the second a howl of protest against the denaturing experience of warfare, much more like the decadent poet Arthur Rimbaud's *A Season in Hell* than anything found in Keats or Wordsworth. It had seemed obvious to many at the outbreak of the First World War that poetry, with its long traditions of celebrating valour, glory, and steadfastness, was the fitting way to approach war. Watson Kerr was only one among many who found that the poetic tools they had inherited were of limited use when it came to bringing the war truthfully home on the printed page.

Samuel Hynes has written in his *A War Imagined* that the First World War was typical of many wars in that it was approached by people whose sole preparation was the past – who went into war armed only with a knowledge based on their reading of earlier wars and on the expectations fostered by their common culture. These were found sadly wanting in the first war, and writers had to conjure new forms in which the terrible truths of this war might enter the wider cultural imagination.

By the time the second war came around the first war had already taken on what Hynes describes as a 'myth' of its own. The writers of the Second World War who had grown up under the shadow of this myth expected a repetition of the static warfare of the First, with its horrors of barbed wire, fixed machine guns, and the relentless pounding of artillery. And they expected a flowering of popular poetry such as had occurred in the First World War. They were disappointed in both expectations, finding themselves in a highly mobile war dominated by the *Blitzkrieg* tactics of aeroplane and tank warfare and a literary landscape in which popular, mass-participative poetry had been eroded by a combination of modernism and the evolution of the new media of film and radio. But the problems of expression, and of coming to terms with war experience remained. The poets of the second war might have had fewer formal impediments to writing directly about war, but the physical and psychological traumas were no less deep.

Edwin Morgan, working as a stretcher-bearer in the desert during the second war, was, for example, haunted by one particular incident: an unexpectedly easy trip with a laden stretcher through clinging sand. It was easy because the officer he was carrying was missing a leg and utterly drained of blood: he was 'light as a child' – 'The New Divan: 99' (162). It took Morgan more than twenty years before he could write directly about that memory.

There was another side to life in the army, however, and in the poem 'The Unspoken' Morgan also remembered the camaraderie of youth and the excitement of travel at that time:

> When the troopship was pitching round the Cape
> in '41, and there was a lull in the night uproar of seas and
>   winds, and a sudden full moon
> swung huge out of the darkness like the world it is,
> and we all crowded onto the wet deck, leaning on the rail,
>   our arms on each other's shoulders, gazing at the
>   savage outcrop of great Africa.[1]

After such moments, despite the bad times, and safely back in civilian life, many young men and women came to realise that they had never lived so fully or so intensely as they did during the war years. In the First World War especially, most men had never been far outside their home village until they were called up and sent to foreign parts. Nor was service in the armed forces exclusively dangerous, for 'hurry up and wait' was the military norm, so that for every hour of action, there would be hundreds of hours of boring routine in the barracks or in reserve behind the line, days in transit, and wild nights on the town.

We should remember, nevertheless, that for every poem, novel or memoir that has been published, from either of the two World Wars, there were hundreds of untold stories remaining in the memories of those who took part. And some of those will be untellable stories, dealing with experiences that could not be spoken of, or brought into the light of day. The American critic Paul Fussell, who fought in France during the second war, has written several books about how war has been represented in the literature and culture of our times, and he suggests that no description of modern war can ever really convey the reality. He notes that however unsparingly realistic the reporting of war may be, in words or visual images, it will never convey the terrible personal impact of the actual experience – of living with the utterly random nature of death, and of seeing how horrendously the human body is mutilated and blown to rags and tatters by modern weapons. The Austrian philosopher Ludwig Wittgenstein sought to raise these limitations on language to the level of philosophy in the seventh and concluding proposition of his *Tractatus Logico-Philosophicus* (1921), written while he was a soldier and then a prisoner in the First World War, stating that 'Whereof one cannot speak, thereof one must be silent.'

Those spared the immediate visual, visceral impacts of the war also experienced something of its unspeakability. To be working in a factory, or on a farm, or in the home was not to be wholly isolated from the consequences of conflict. To find oneself in a context of universal uncertainty, when one battle or catastrophic air raid might change a communal or personal future irrevocably, or a telegram rip apart one's family forever, is not to feel safely out of the way. To have to endure the loss of a loved one in a faraway place, with no body and no known burial place to grieve over, and then to have to live with that memory and all the obligations to the dead that entail is to be saved from only the most immediately horrific elements of war. But it is to experience all of war's crushing alienation, the sense of powerlessness and insignificance that it inflicts on all those it treads down in its remorseless progress, and it is to feel, too, the helplessness that conspires to drown out the individual voice in what seems an overwhelming deluge of the suffering of others.

So war poetry, the making of *poems* about war, may be both a contradiction and a kind of triumph. The very act of making a potentially lyrical art out of such loss and suffering might seem to be at best insensitive, and at worst disrespectful of the dead. How do we write about what modern war is really like? And yet how can we not write about it? The artist's job, after all, has always been to bear witness, and the best art has always expanded our understanding of what it is to be human in inspiring but also, alas, in dismaying ways. So we might ask the question, can the poetry of war be 'lyrical' at all? Perhaps it should take the epic form, longer, more distanced, stark and bare in its utterance, as Homer did for the matter of Troy. David Jones took up something of this challenge in his long poem, *In Parenthesis* (1937), which infused his own experience of the First World War, with references to ancient myth and the historical past.

Most of the poets in this study, however, have chosen the lyric, the short poem of personal feeling, as the most appropriate response to the pressures of the times. And indeed, this has remained the first choice of many modern poets, ever since the Romantic poetry of Coleridge and especially Wordsworth, who saw no contradiction in combining personal feeling with a strong social conscience.

The literature of the First World War, and especially the poetry of Wilfred Owen and Siegfried Sassoon, has moved

Scottish War Poetry 1914–1945 7

us all with its power and its compassion, and indeed their poems have significantly influenced our understanding of that conflict and dictated how most of us have come to feel about it. It seems to have defined what 'war poetry' might be. Owen was killed seven days before the Great War came to an end and, in the preface to a collection of poems that he never lived to see published, he made the following memorable statement:

> This book is not about heroes. English poetry is not yet fit to speak of them.
> Nor is it about deeds, or lands, nor anything about glory, honour, might, majesty, dominion, or power, except War.
> Above all I am not concerned with Poetry.
> My subject is War, and the pity of War.
> The Poetry is in the pity.
> Yet these elegies are to this generation in no sense consolatory. They may be to the next. All a poet can do today is warn. That is why the true Poets must be truthful.[2]

Reading their work, we are rightly moved by the pity, rage and pain expressed by the poets of the first war, who seem to be speaking for a whole generation who felt betrayed by the very civilisation they were told they were fighting for. 'Never such innocence' wrote Philip Larkin, many years later, thinking of that early rush of patriotic enlistment, 'Never such innocence again.'[3]

Nevertheless, Owen, like so many of his generation, still believed in the concept of Christian sacrifice even amidst, perhaps especially amidst, the carnage of the trenches – something he shares with Scottish poets as diverse as Roderick Watson Kerr, John Buchan, and John MacDougall Hay. One of Owen's poems is called 'Greater Love', after all, and his verses echo with images of the Christ-like sacrifice being undertaken by the men around him. Here is what he said in a letter to Osbert Sitwell on 4 July 1918, only four months before he was killed:

> For 14 hours yesterday I was at work – teaching Christ to lift his cross by numbers, and how to adjust his crown [...] I attended his Supper to see that there were no complaints; and inspected his feet that they should be worthy of the nails. I see to it that he is dumb, and stands at attention before his accusers. With a piece of silver I buy him every day, and with maps I make him familiar with the topography of Golgotha.

By comparison, the tub-thumping verses of patriotic propaganda that appeared in 1914 by the likes of MacKenzie MacBride and Charles Murray are a less admirable kind of writing, although they too have their place as a historical record of the spirit of the times and must not be forgotten. Tennyson's poem 'The Charge of the Light Brigade' could cry 'honour the Light Brigade, / Noble six hundred' without a trace of irony in 1854, barely two months after what was already suspected to be an infamous blunder. Such a position would be unthinkable today, but we should not forget that in 1914 Rupert Brooke had welcomed the prospect of war, as a glorious challenge for his generation, that had –

> wakened us from sleeping,
> With hand made sure, clear eye, and sharpened power,
> To turn, as swimmers into cleanness leaping,
> Glad from a world grown old and cold and weary.[4]

He was not alone in such feelings, for cheering crowds gathered outside Buckingham Palace when war was declared. Only four years later, however, everything was changed and nothing could be quite the same again. According to Paul Fussell, 'modern memory' would never think of war again, without a strong sense of terrible irony.

Scottish War Poetry 1914–1945

Owen claimed that the poetry was in the pity, and this raises questions about exactly what we are studying when we read 'war poetry'. It may well be that for many readers the emotional impact and historical significance of these extraordinary poems has as much or more to do with the ghastly events being described, and the pathos of the poet's presence, as it has to do with the actual poetry. Is it the poetry or the pity that is moving us? Is 'pity' enough, when our response might just as easily be 'anger', followed by a stronger and much more critical focus on the political and economic factors that lead countries into war? Can pity and rage coexist in the same poem, and how constructive are such emotions, once invoked?

Such tensions are not necessarily destructive. In fact we can witness an evolution in poetic form in many of the poems from both wars here discussed, as the best poets find that regular rhythms and formal rhyme schemes seem less and less appropriate to their chosen subject. Or perhaps the struggle to express complex and painful feelings that almost defy expression has released so many tensions that any more formally elegant plan to the poem has simply broken up under the pressure. See, for example, the shortened lines, the stripped-down language, and the insistently repeated crude couplet rhymes of Roderick Watson Kerr's first-war poem 'Denial' (30). Compare, too, a very similar tension in G. S. Fraser's poem 'S.S. *City of Benares*' (100), from 1940, with a similar use of insistent rhyme, in a syntax that seems to be buckling and twisting under the force of the poet's despair.

In the 1920s, Bertolt Brecht was suspicious of writers who sought to raise strong feeling in their dramatic art, for he wanted his theatre audiences to *think* in a much more political way about what they were seeing. So he introduced 'distancing effects' to his plays, using ironic songs, and placards in the wings, to break the illusion of realism and to break the emotional spell of the moment on stage. His aim was to raise the political consciousness of his audiences in ways that might lead them, not to tears, but to action in the real world beyond the stage.

Lyric feeling should not be underestimated, however, even when the moment in question is itself beyond all common experience, and almost beyond artistic expression. The various poems in this study each find their own, and different solutions to the challenge. Thus the tortured poems by Roderick Watson Kerr and G. S. Fraser re-enact grief, rage and trauma with their stresses and pauses, their use of alliteration and rhyme, their smooth or ugly rhythms, their broken or convoluted syntax. On the other hand, the measured calmness and the quiet decency and pathos of Violet Jacob's 'The Field by the Lirk o' the Hill' (24), and Flora Garry's 'Ambulance Depot 1942' (107), take a very different route, whose understated dignity is an equally powerful and unforgettable reminder of the true face of war.

Such is the legacy of the many poems discussed in this study.

THE FIRST WORLD WAR: 1914–1918
THE PATTERN OF EXPECTATION

It is one of the truisms of history that military generals are always preparing to fight not the next war, but the previous one. This is an argument that has often been applied to Britain's participation in the First World War: that in 1914 the British Army embarked on a conflict that would come to be characterised by the industrial carnage of machine guns, barbed wire, and naval blockade with a mindset formed on colonial-era cavalry charges and naïve and outdated notions of honour and glory.

This, like many truisms, is in fact a gross oversimplification. But it speaks to something profound about the nature of war itself – that no matter how much one has prepared for war, or how hard one has attempted to anticipate its effects, each war comes as a profound, unprecedented shock. When it comes to conflict we have only the past as a guide, and war in the twentieth and twenty-first centuries has shown a frightening capacity to outstrip people's previous experiences and sometimes even their wildest imaginings.

In this way at least, the First World War was arguably the most shocking of the many wars of the twentieth century. As the awful horrors of the Battle of Loos in 1915, and the Battles of the Somme in 1916 and Passchendaele in 1917 were revealed, it became clear that the British military and the British public had come to this conflict terribly underprepared: that there was a huge gap between their expectation of what war might bring and its devastating, unforeseen consequences.

This was a social problem, but it was also a literary one, for literature had played a significant part in forming the pattern of expectation preceding war. As Paul Fussell has shown in his foundational work *The Great War and Modern Memory*, the population of Great Britain entered the war bolstered and encouraged by a strong literary tradition of both pastoral and martial poetry that defined and celebrated what Shakespeare had characterised three centuries before as 'this sceptered isle':

> This earth of majesty, this seat of Mars,
> This other Eden, demi-paradise,
> This fortress built by Nature for her self
> Against infection and the hand of war,
> This happy breed of men, this little world,
> This precious stone set in a silver sea
> Which serves it in the office of a wall
> Or as a moat defensive to a house,
> Against the envy of less happier lands
> (*Richard II*, 2, 1, ll. 41–9)

The First World War was effectively the first large-scale European war to be fought in an era of universal literacy and the last before the advent of sound film, radio, and television. As such, the written word had a power and a reach that it would never have again. Written journalism mattered, popular fiction mattered, the literary tradition mattered, and poetry mattered. The kinds of sentiments about British insularity, closeness to nature, yet cheerful and resolute bravery in the face of threats from continental Europe described by Shakespeare, had become an important staple in the literature through which British children had been educated in the half century before the war. When, as Samuel Hynes noted in his *A War Imagined*, the British population attempted to conceive of the coming war in 1914 it was often to these models that it resorted.

Scotland was, of course, a special case. Many readers will note that Shakespeare's words, written before the Union of the Crowns in 1603 and the Union of 1707 and set in the context of the late medieval period, were really about types of Englishness rather than a post-dated Britishness. But the war also marked what was probably the closest moment of Scottish cultural and political integration into the United Kingdom. The British Empire was just about to reach its greatest extent and the Scots had played a significant role in its development, willingly conforming to an imperial economy, a politics, and a culture that brought the nation both considerable wealth and also a nuanced recognition of its status as a significant partner in the twin projects of union and empire. Under such conditions Shakespeare was, like Bunyan and Wordsworth and Dickens, willingly accepted and appreciated in Scotland as a British rather than narrowly English writer, while correspondingly Scottish writers such as Burns and Scott, Stevenson and Barrie, were regarded as important contributors to a hybrid but unified British identity.

The idea of an independent Scottish literature had, through the agency of works of literary history such as T. F. Henderson's *Scottish Vernacular Literature* (1898) and J. H. Millar's *A Literary History of Scotland* (1903), come to be seen as one that had only a historical application: a notion that would be reinforced in the immediate aftermath of the war with the publication of George Gregory Smith's *Scottish Literature: Character and Influence* (1919). The idea propounded by Gregory Smith, that a distinctive independent Scottish literature had effectively ceased to exist by the middle of the nineteenth century, is increasingly being challenged by modern scholars, but it is indicative of the attitudes towards a national literary culture that prevailed at the time of the First World War. As such, most Scots were content to embrace a wider British culture and identify with and take their inspiration from the works of the English literary tradition.

The extent to which individual Scots could draw inspiration from that tradition can be seen in two contrasting individuals. John Buchan was already a successful novelist, journalist, and publisher before the war and would become effectively the head of the British propaganda effort for a large part of its duration. Davie Kirkwood was a trade union organiser and a member of the influential Clyde Workers Committee who was considered so potentially disruptive to the war effort that he was forcibly deported from his sphere of operations in Glasgow in 1916 (albeit only as far as Edinburgh). As their autobiographies – Kirkwood's *My Life of* Revolt (1935) and Buchan's *Memory Hold-the-Door* (1940) – testify, though, each felt the distinctive values of conscience and fidelity on which they based their life work had been formed on the same book: Bunyan's *Pilgrim's Progress*.

Serving soldiers also felt the inspiration of the English literary tradition, sometimes strongly, and felt it useful both as consolation and inspiration in offering models on which they might build their understanding of war and pattern their response to it. Alexander Douglas Gillespie from Linlithgow, a young Second Lieutenant in the Argyll and Sutherland Highlanders, was one such. Gillespie was killed in 1915 on the first day of the Battle of Loos, the first catastrophic blooding of the Scottish soldiers who had volunteered the previous year in Lord Kitchener's New Army. As his collected *Letters from Flanders* (1916) tells us, among Gillespie's effects that were returned to his family from France was found his copy of *Pilgrim's Progress* marked at the page which read: 'Then I entered into the Valley of the Shadow of Death, and had no light, for almost half the way through it. I thought I should have been killed there, over and over; but at last day broke, and the sun rose, and I went through that which was behind with far more ease and quiet.' As Paul Fussell has noted, Gillespie had also written movingly to his father on the eve of battle, knowing well the strong possibility of his death in the morning but drawing inspiration and hope from another canonical English writer:

It will be a great fight, and even when I think of you, I would not wish to be out of this. You remember Wordsworth's 'Happy Warrior':

> who if he be called upon to face
> Some awful moment to which heaven has joined
> Great issues, good or bad, for human kind,
> Is happy as a lover, and is attired
> With sudden brightness like a man inspired.

Well, I never could be all that a happy warrior should be, but it will please you to know that I am very happy, and whatever happens you will remember that.[5]

To a sophisticated modern reader – a reader acquainted with the horrors of the First and Second World Wars and with those of the organised and disorganised conflicts that have followed – the sentiments of Wordsworth's poem may seem hopelessly conventional and trite in its invocations of all the many things that a Happy Warrior should wish to be and its easy 'confidence of Heaven's applause'. Wordsworth had not fought in a war nor seen at first hand the awful things people can do to each other in the name of honour or duty or glory. Yet here was a young man with military experience speaking with a strong assurance of his imminent death, for whom Wordsworth's words encapsulated an aspiration and a set of values worth sacrificing his life for.

Gillespie was only one of many British – and Scottish – soldiers who found in Shakespeare, The King James Bible, *Pilgrim's Progress*, and poems like Wordsworth's 'Happy Warrior', Burns's 'Scots Wha Ha'e', and Tennyson's 'The Charge of the Light Brigade' a rich source of moral inspiration, but also ways of conceptualising warfare and of understanding their duties to their nation through it.

There was a recent tradition too, characterised by the more overtly popular poetry of Rudyard Kipling and Henry Newbolt, that had in recent years added an emphatic imperialist dimension to this tradition. Kipling had, in the poems of *Barrack-Room Ballads* (1892) and the short stories in collections such as *Soldiers Three* (1888), created less idealised versions of British martial writing – adding both racial hybridity and dialect voice to the mix while still retaining a strong sense of duty to nation, empire, and to what he called 'the Law' that binds the individual to the values of the collective. His *Barrack-Room Ballads* offered a more realistic account of army life in the outposts of empire, employing the forms that had been popularised by the Scottish Border Ballads to depict the ways in which those often seen at the margins – Irish, Cockneys, Scots – played their understated parts in upholding the values of Britain and its empire. Kipling's poetry was rhythmical and employed strong, simple rhymes, driving his message along with the force of an army on the march. A poem such as 'Tommy' seeks to highlight the hypocrisy of civilians who make 'mock o' uniforms that guard you while you sleep', looking down on soldiers while ignoring the protections they offer. But it does this in a form that manufactures a kind of consent from the reader for the subject: speaking in a common language with an easily gettable rhythm, repetitions, and predictable rhymes, and thus seeming to appeal to values we all hold in common:

> We aren't no thin red 'eroes, nor we aren't no blackguards too,
> But single men in barricks, most remarkable like you;
> An' if sometimes our conduck isn't all your fancy paints:
> Why, single men in barricks don't grow into plaster saints;
>
> While it's Tommy this, an' Tommy that, an' Tommy, fall be'ind,'
> But it's 'Please to walk in front, sir,' when there's trouble in the wind,

Scottish War Poetry 1914–1945   17

>There's trouble in the wind, my boys, there's trouble in the
>wind,
>O it's 'Please to walk in front, sir,' when there's trouble in
>the wind.

Henry Newbolt's 'Vitaï Lampada' (1897), is rather more patrician in tone and refined in language, comparing the experience of war to a public-school cricket match. Yet it too deploys an easy, almost simplistic, rhythm and rhyme, and a repeating refrain of 'Play up! play up! and play the game!' in order to convince its readers of a stable communal identity – a team ethos – founded on the relationship between good fellowship, duty, and national honour:

>The sand of the desert is sodden red, –
>Red with the wreck of a square that broke; –
>The Gatling's jammed and the Colonel dead,
>And the regiment blind with dust and smoke.
>The river of death has brimmed his banks,
>And England's far, and Honour a name,
>But the voice of schoolboy rallies the ranks,
>'Play up! play up! and play the game!'

THE ANTICIPATION OF WAR

Given the popularity of such works, alongside others that dealt with soldiering and death, such as A. E. Housman's *A Shropshire Lad* (1896) – another work deeply influenced by the Border Ballads – it is hardly surprising to find that much of the early writing of the war, both north and south of the border, modelled itself on the literary patterns established by these late-Victorian and Edwardian precedents.

One such example is 'The Border Breed' by **R. W. Campbell** (13), published in his collection *The Making of Micky McGhee: And Other Stories in Verse* (1916). In both its title and its use of poetic form, Campbell's book clearly shows the influence of Kipling, and of the poems of Yukon prospecting penned by the Scotsman known as 'the Canadian Kipling', Robert Service. 'The Border Breed' acknowledges its debt to Kipling and the English tradition in its first line, before illustrating that poetic influence in both its form and its language:

> I crave for the style of Kipling, the touch that Tennyson made,
> To write of the Border gallants who served in a Scots Brigade,
> Men of the hills and snowdrifts – men of the weaver's spool,
> Called, and of one ambition, to die like the Border School,
> A thousand sons of bold Reivers who dreamed of the Battle Yards,
> Where bonnets and blades were headed by brave McSteele from the Guards.

In formal terms, Campbell follows the variation of ballad form used by Kipling in poems like 'Tommy' above. The conventional ballad form usually employs alternating lines of eight and six syllables, an iambic tetrameter followed by an iambic trimeter, with rhymes occurring at the end of the trimeter in an abcb rhyme scheme. Kipling takes these tetrameters and trimeters and runs them into one fourteen-syllable iambic line – a heptameter – that is generally punctuated or paused around halfway after the seventh or eighth syllable, and then rhymed in couplets. Campbell's poem adopts this form and employs it in his poem (with a more definite break after the eighth syllable) in an attempt to achieve the reassuring rhythmical effects of the ballad with all its traditional associations with narratives of derring-do and tragedy.

By taking this form, and reminding us explicitly of the reiving traditions of skirmish and confrontation from which it comes, Campbell sets the reader up to receive a modern variant of border ballad transposed to the First World War, in this case the campaign against the Turks at Gallipoli. As the poem progresses it demonstrates many of the benefits of this popular form, describing vividly the action of battle, for example, in a driving, rhythmical verse:

> When the song of the guns had ended, McSteele yelled,
>   'Charge!' and well
> He led them through shrieking shrapnel and a zipping
>   Dum-dum Hell.

But the allusions to the ballad tradition also bring with them an expectation of tragedy. Ballads rarely end happily. And so, in this poem the reader knows almost from the beginning that its hero 'brave MacSteele' will not survive. His demise comes predictably, and with an equally predictable 'Alas!', at the moment of glorious failure:

> They reached the third of the trenches. Alas! this third
>   was a scrape
> Of earth that duped air observers, and sent brave
>   McSteele to his fate.
> So, seeking for their objective, these braves were lured to
>   a fire
> That staggered, murdered and mangled, and caused the
>   order – 'Retire!'
> From out of a thousand heroes a hundred limped to the
>   rear,
> Bleeding, battered, and broken – minus the Chief without fear.
>
> There's gloom on the hills of the Borders, gloom by the
>   shuttle and loom,
> For McSteele and his missing gallants – and 'missing' is
>   mainly doom.

No praises are printed in papers – no praises are wanted
   or asked,
For duty's the creed of the Hillmen, Death they expect in
   the task.
*Oh, Britons, thank God for the Borders! Thank God for the
   men who parade,
Square-jawed, grim, dour, and determined, in a far-off
   Lowland Brigade!*

Where this poem develops away from the ballad tradition is in the editorial that closes the poem, which has a rather intrusive effect and points its moral a little too sharply: turning a stirring, tragic tale into something that bears an uncomfortable resemblance to propaganda. The ballad voice is a popular voice, its narrator giving the impression of being at one with the people and the action it describes. By moving away from this and employing a direct mode of address to the national community of readers, the poem loses this character of speaking about the people on behalf of the people and seems to become instead the mouthpiece of a coercive establishment.

This sense in which poetry is not simply creating a pattern of expectation of what war might be like but actively attempting to shape behaviour – to encourage and enforce the proper ways to respond to the war – was a feature of much of the early poetry of the war. In the English context, one of the most celebrated poems of this kind is Rupert Brooke's sonnet 'The Soldier', written at the end of 1914. At one level the poem is a haunting example of proleptic elegy – the imagining of what a future loss might feel like – as well as a moving personal statement of fidelity, courage, and love of homeland:

If I should die, think only this of Me:
That there's some corner of a foreign field
That is for ever England. There shall be
In that rich earth a richer dust concealed;

A dust whom England bore, shaped, made aware,
Gave, once, her flowers to love, her ways to roam,
A body of England's, breathing English air,
Washed by the rivers, blest by suns of home.

But as many readers have also noted, the frequent repetition of 'England' and 'English' (employed six times in the sonnet's fourteen lines) imbues the poem with what is perhaps an unwonted emphasis on national values, threatening to turn a meditation on the pity of war into an unwitting encouragement for others to follow the example of Brooke's soldier in the name of national honour. Brooke's poem emphasises the peacefulness of death in war (which is perhaps rather problematic in itself) and the reconciliation of the dead soldier with the land that nurtured him, concluding with a description of 'hearts at peace, under an English heaven'. But as the many propagandists who took up the poem showed, it also lent itself to a reading that used its implicit patriotism as a spur to goad waverers into enlisting in order to defend the national values it invoked.

Scotland had, of course, a proud martial tradition and so it is unsurprising to find examples of Scottish poets drawing on that tradition and on examples of national independence and unity of purpose to write what was effectively a form of recruiting propaganda. A rather simplistic version of this came from the pen of **MacKenzie MacBride** in his 'Shouther Airms!' (38). MacBride was a popular commercial writer who had written potboiling works like *Wonderfu' Weans* (1903) and *Arran of the Bens, the Glens and the Brave* (1910), and his poem arguably continues this unsophisticated celebratory tone. As such it is typical of many of the poems that appeared in Scottish newspapers in the early months of the war.

Like these poems it uses a regular metrical scheme to deliver its message of national unity and martial pride. If a poem such as this is about the bringing together of diversity – with each of its three stanzas speaking in a first-person plural voice on behalf of three distinct areas of Scotland: the Lowlands, the Borders, and the Highlands – and reinforcing in its fourth stanza that old Scots saying that 'we're a' Jock Tamson's bairns', then what better way could there be to enforce the unity than by employing a regular, homogenising form and series of easy rhymes. MacBride's formal choices – three quatrains of regular abba rhyme each speaking for a distinct region, followed by a fourth similar quatrain introduced with the exhortation 'All together' – effectively melds all the voices into one, with the implication that we are of one mind on the issue of Scottish duty in the face of war: 'All together – / Kissens all o' "Tamson's" race'. Dialect has an important part to play in this too, reinforcing the references to the traditional markers of Scottish military experience, the kilt and the pipes, with a linguistic marker that unites Scotland internally while emphasising its distinctiveness within the larger war effort. In this way Scotland is showing itself more than willing to join in the larger allied war effort, while carefully guarding the distinctiveness of the contribution that it makes.

A more subtle version, but nonetheless equally loaded, version of these ideas can be found in **Charles Murray**'s 'A Sough o' War' (62). Murray was a native of Aberdeenshire, long-settled in South Africa when the war broke out in 1914. Although an economic exile he wrote extensively about the North East of Scotland in a vigorous, authentic regional dialect, and played an important part in the Doric revival that began to gain pace during the war. 'A Sough o' War' begins, a little like Brooke's 'Soldier' by evoking in idyllic fashion a landscape and a way of life that demands of our honour that we defend it:

> The corn was turnin', hairst was near,
>   But lang afore the scythes could start
> A sough o' war gaed through the land

An' stirred it to its benmost heart.
Nae ours the blame, but when it came
We couldna pass the challenge by,
For credit o' our honest name
There could be but the ae reply.
An' buirdly men, fae strath an' glen,
An' shepherds fae the bucht an' hill,
Will show them a', whate'er befa',
Auld Scotland counts for something still.

By the careful use of long vowel sounds in the first two lines, Murray evokes (like Keats before him) the sleepy, ripened feel of 'hairst' – harvest-time – and treats the rumour of war – the 'sough' – as like a natural breath of wind sighing its vague, ominous threat across the land. The response is at first reluctance, 'Nae ours the blame', and then resolution, 'but when it cam / We couldna pass the challenge by', which leads very quickly into a more aggressive statement of action and assertion of national pride. Within five lines, the poem has moved from reluctant defence to passionate advocacy of Scottish values.

The last two lines of this first stanza are particularly interesting, in part because of the boast that 'Auld Scotland counts for something still' – which reappears as a refrain throughout the rest of the poem – but also because of the slightly prickly ambivalence that introduces and perhaps even undermines it. The assertion that the bold and 'buirdly' countrymen 'Will show them a'' seems emphatic; but is also ambiguous as the object of this assertion, the 'them' whom we'll show, remains undefined. The implication that it's not just the Germans but also the English who will get this timely reminder that Scotland matters, is reinforced in the second stanza. Here the poem moves to the 'gallant loons' from 'brochs an' toons' who it asserts are 'keen to show baith friend an' foe / Auld Scotland counts for something still.' There is perhaps something characteristically Scottish in this combination of assertive braggadocio and defensive prickliness: a slightly resentful realisation that we are habituated to seeing ourselves as others see us in ways that might never occur to the likes of Brooke with his complacent assurance of 'an English heaven'.

Murray's poem's regular form, its relentless pattern of iambic tetrameters and use of simple, emphatic rhyme, comes into its own in its final stanza when it reveals itself fully as a piece of exhortatory recruiting propaganda, calling on young and old to answer the call:

> The grim, grey fathers, bent wi' years,
>   Come stridin' through the muirland mist,
> Wi' beardless lads scarce by wi' school
>   But eager as the lave to list.
> We've fleshed o' yore the braid claymore
>   On mony a bloody field afar,
> But ne'er did skirlin' pipes afore
>   Cry on sae urgently to war.
>   Gin danger's there, we'll thole our share,
>   Gie's but the weapons, we've the will,
>   Ayont the main, to prove again
>   Auld Scotland counts for something still.

Like MacBride's poem, 'A Sough o' War' draws on the imagery of the martial tradition – 'the braid claymore', the 'skirlin' pipes' – not just to instil in its Scottish readers a pride in their national heritage but to use that past to encourage them to enlist.

A strong element in many types of propagandistic war verse is the attempt to build continuity, to insist on a kind of social contract or network of obligation between the dead and the living, with the implication that when we are dead we will be remembered in like fashion: we are obliged to honour the great actions of the past in order for our own great actions to be honoured in the future. MacBride and Murray both play on that sense, drawing on the patterns of the past in an attempt to shape the future. As such, it makes a great deal of sense for them to employ verse forms and a diction that draw upon a common stock of experience, reminding us by those patterns that we are showing faith not just with one another in the present but also with our common past.

POETRY GOES TO WAR

What happens, though, if, as has been suggested earlier, the anticipated future refuses to conform to the shape of the past, when war on such an unprecedented scale exceeds the comprehension of traditional methods? The poems we have looked at so far idealise warfare as a means to encourage recruiting. The poetry we look at in the next section explores what happened when individuals found themselves at the sharp end of modern war and discovered some gaping holes between that idealisation and actuality.

Pre-war and early-war writing was not all like the poems of MacBride and Murray already discussed, although they are quite typical of the very many poems that appeared in the press at the outbreak of hostilities. Alongside the mass-media that had developed rapidly in Scotland, as elsewhere, from the 1890s, there was an alternative press, much smaller in scale, but vocal and influential. One of the foremost examples was the weekly paper *Forward*, published in Glasgow by the Independent Labour Party. The paper had been a strong advocate of women's suffrage before the war and strongly opposed the decision to go to war in 1914. It bolstered this position by publishing a range of anti-war poetry in the early months of the conflict, typical of which is 'Speak not to me of War!' by **William Cameron** (17).

In many ways this offers a mirror image of poems like MacBride's, employing the same kinds of abstraction in describing war, talking of it in terms of 'strife', and of honour as a 'scroll of fame', and employing metonyms like 'sword' and 'gun' to describe action, as well as inversions of normal syntax, for example 'Speak not to me'. It employs, too, a kind of conventional poetic diction in which people do such things as 'Laud' each other and point to things 'yonder'. Such a conventional note is struck in the evocation of grief that begins 'See yonder lonely woman weep'. This might be seen as a worthy attempt to ground the abstraction of war in a particular emotional moment – an opportunity to witness the impact of war on a grieving mother – but the poem seems unable to escape a sentimentalising gloss in its appeal to the reader's pity, drawing on a rather tired stock of images in its description of the 'heartfelt silent tear' that 'slowly trickles down her cheek'. And the poem does all this in a highly conventional form, a ballad metre with alternating iambic tetrameters and trimeters and a rigid pattern of abab rhyme.

What is clearly different, however, is the poem's overall argument and tone. It would be difficult to fit descriptions of butchery and phrases like 'bloody corpse-strewn pain' into poems such as MacBride's and Murray's, which suggests that there is a strong degree of irony in Cameron's use of militaristic euphemisms. Cameron's poem is plainly using such euphemisms to undermine the notions of Glory that are characteristically employed by those who support war and encourage young people to take a part in it. Cameron sets up quite deliberately a contrast between the conventional poetic language of warfare, heard in poems by the likes of Wordsworth, Tennyson, or Newbolt, and more realistic and graphic images of a 'corpse-strewn' battlefield and soldiers who have been 'butchered' by others. There is still, arguably, something rather 'poetic' and conventional in these descriptions – a 'corpse-strewn plain' is an image from the poetic imagination rather than from the eye of one who has witnessed the horrors of war at first hand, and there is something rather abstract in the generalising use of 'man' in the phrase 'where man has butchered man' that suggests that Cameron is still unable to see war wholly free from conventional blinkers. It is difficult to know, too, whether the poem employs a conventional form in order to interrogate and undermine the patriotic verse rhetoric of Kipling and Newbolt or because Cameron simply assumes that poems must take these kinds of shapes – that it is the job of poetry, and even a poetry that seeks to undermine conventional assumptions, to speak always in a measured, regular, ordered manner.

The same cannot be said of another poem from the early war period, 'All the Hills and Vales Along' by **Charles Hamilton Sorley** (77), which uses many conventional poetic usages – a regular metronomic rhythm, simple rhymes, and song-like refrain – in a way that is surely intended to be bitterly ironic. Unlike Cameron, Sorley wrote this poem while in uniform, having volunteered at the outbreak of war, and so he wrote the poem out of a direct experience of conflict, even though warfare is not directly mentioned in it.

Sorley's poem seems less immediately rhetorical than Cameron's. Where Cameron establishes his anti-war opinions by using contrasts and then direct contradiction of established views, Sorley simply makes several pertinent observations that make the rhetoric of war-mongers seem increasingly absurd. The first stanza's apparent assurances of the cheerfulness of stoical troops going gladly to war, like a regiment of happy warriors, is subtly undercut even from its beginning. The second couplet, with its easy rhyming of the informal 'chaps' and 'going to die perhaps' has a sardonic quality that comes from the almost comic inappropriateness of the matching of these two ideas. This establishes a sense of uneasiness in the poem, a sense that the jaunty sing-song assurances bestowed by the form and the simple unsophisticated language do not quite match the serious implications of the poem's subject matter.

Sorley reinforces this by destabilising the ideas on which Brooke's 'Soldier' is founded: that nature somehow bestows a blessing and the consolation of remembrance on those who fight in its defence. Sorley's first stanza asks the soldiers to trust in nature and to 'Give your gladness to earth's keeping, / So be glad, when you are sleeping', and in its second offers the bland assurance that 'Teeming earth will surely store / All the gladness that you pour'. But as the poem progresses it becomes clear that such conventionalised assurances are worthless, and that we are in effect foolish if we believe nature is anything other than indifferent to both the sufferings and joys of human life. As the poem's third stanza makes increasingly clear, nature hasn't just survived at cataclysmic moments of human history such as the deaths of the founders of the Christian religion and the Western philosophic tradition – it has thrived. The hemlock that poisoned Socrates was borne 'with joyful ease' from the earth, and the ground beneath Christ's cross 'blossomed and was glad', just as it will 'rejoice and blossom' in its careless way when the singing soldiers go into it as corpses.

The use of the refrain – wholly appropriate in a poem that is about soldiers singing – becomes increasingly ironic as the poem develops and we see the gap between its cheerful form and the bleak prospects of the singing soldiers it portrays. The inclusion in the final stanza of two additional lines to the refrain, making a six-line chorus that contrasts with the four-line choruses used in the first three stanzas, is a particularly clever, and perhaps cruel, invention. The first two lines 'On, marching men, on, / To the gates of death with song', with their relentlessness and their use of an imperative, hectoring voice, suggest that these are not so much individuals cementing their solidarity by means of a jaunty route march as a group being impelled relentlessly and remorselessly to their graves. Their cheerfulness and stoicism is admirable, perhaps, but we are made aware that it will do nothing to avert the deaths that await, or soften the indifference of the cosmos to them. The nature that Sorley evokes in this closing stanza is quite different from that depicted by Romantic poetry and by Brooke, serving not as consoling manifestation of divine order but as a booming echo-chamber reflecting back in its emptiness the folly of human hopes: 'So be merry, so be dead'.

Sorley's use of highly conventional forms, employed and exaggerated here to point up the absurdity of the ways in which war has been traditionally depicted in poetry, is one way of dealing with the problem many soldier poets found in trying to match their new experiences to established forms. In employing a heavy irony Sorley is conforming to a mode that Paul Fussell has argued is the dominant response of many of the war's soldiers – highlighting the great gap between all the official discourses war throws up and the much less elevated ways in which it is experienced.

Such irony can be found expressed in a slightly different manner in 'The Sniper' by **W. D. Cocker** (18). 'The Sniper' is much more conversational in its tone, employing a more relaxed, less insistent scheme of iambic pentameter that allows for some metrical variation – not the least in the cleverly crafted fifth line, which emphasises the abruptness of the soldier's death by the use a shortened line with two spondees (two-stressed disyllabic feet), 'By Jove' and 'got him', on either side of the 'I'. The longer line length used consistently in the other lines makes the poem's rhymes less emphatic than they are in the seven-syllable lines of 'All the Hills and Vales Along', even though it employs a regular abab scheme (with, again, a slight variation in the first five lines). Cocker's word choice is also noticeably less formal and less obviously poetic with few of the inversions and poeticisms we have seen in the work of Brooke or Cameron. Lines such as 'He raised his rifle, took quick aim and shot him. / Two hundred yards away the man dropped dead' have the directness and terseness of a prose account, and are far removed from the poeticism of Cameron's 'yonders' or Brooke's 'dust whom England bore'.

'The Sniper' is above all else, an ironic work. And this irony works in two ways. Firstly there is a dramatic irony that allows the reader to see the reality that is hidden from the sniper himself. Pleased at the achievement of registering a hit and gaining (in one of the work's few poetic formulations) the 'meed of praise' from his comrades, the sniper is oblivious to the consequences of his act. The poem makes sure, though, that the reader is not. And it does this in a complex way, taking us beyond the fairly conventional pathos created by the image of the weeping mother or wife that proved sufficient for Cameron's poem, to a more thoughtful speculation on the remorse and the anguish the sniper might feel were he to realise fully what he has done. The fact that he doesn't feel this, though, is not put down to his callousness or inhumanity. The poem is careful to tell us that he would, if he understood the grief he has caused, be haunted by it in his 'every dream' and 'all his thoughts by night and day'. In this way, the poem brings home to us one of the truly awful aspects of warfare: not that it is the result of bad people doing wilfully wicked things to one another, but rather that it is the consequence of people just like you or me who find themselves placed in circumstances in which they inflict pain and sorrow unwittingly and unwontedly on others.

This first irony is reinforced by a further one in the final line, which turns the poem on its head. This time it is a cosmic irony, employed to make the reader realise the futility of war in the larger scale of things. The implication in the poem's last line, that it could equally well be one of 'ours' killed rather than one of 'theirs' and that the soldiers of different nations are in effect interchangeable (cruelly reinforced by the italicised statement that *'It's all the same'*, and the use of

Scottish War Poetry 1914–1945 31

brackets that make it seem almost a throwaway line) conveys a similar message about the overwhelming folly of war made in Sorley's poem. In different ways, each poem creates an ironic distance between their protagonists and the reader in an effort to show how inadequate conventional attitudes and ways of representing war are when faced with the complicated, often pitiless reality.

THE WAR WITH FORM

Much of the Scottish – and British – poetry by combatants in the First World War could be said, like these poems, to be engaged in a battle with poetic form: to be finding in its attempts to render truly the full range of the new experience thrown up by war that it was straining against the patterns established by the conventions of language, metre, and rhyme that it had inherited. In a larger context, this is exactly the problem that the contemporaneous literary and artistic movements of modernism sought to find an answer to – how to find new, satisfactory ways to render the unprecedented complications of modern, urban, technological life. For modernist painters, this manifested itself in a desire to break free from the studio and the academy and experiment with light and colour and perspective, employing all the techniques of abstraction to shake spectators out of their assumptions that art should be representational and apparently realistic in its conventions. For writers, modernism offered analogous kinds of experimentation: encouraging poets to break with the conventions of rhyme, metre, and poetic language and experiment with fragmented, discordant images; and allowing prose writers the freedom to explore inner states of consciousness and irrationality through bold new techniques such as stream of consciousness narration.

Very few of those who wrote about war in Scotland, or in Britain more widely, could be described as modernists in quite these terms. The most celebrated modernists of the period – in poetry W. B. Yeats, T. S. Eliot, and Ezra Pound, and in prose Marcel Proust, James Joyce, and Virginia Woolf – all in their different ways kept the war very much at a distance from their work. Instead, war writers, tended to find themselves engaged in a battle with convention rather than in repudiating it entirely. Wilfred Owen's attempts to encapsulate the pity and terror of war found him not breaking with rhyme altogether, but rather experimenting with techniques such as half-rhyme to suggest the derangement of war. Siegfried Sassoon, similarly wrote impassioned, angry poems that described the futility and despair of the war but almost always did so in perfectly rhymed stanzas and well-turned sonnets.

The Scottish academic and poet, **Archibald Allan Bowman**, also wrote extensively in the sonnet form, most notably in his *Sonnets from a Prison Camp* (1919). The Prussian military theorist, Claus von Clausewitz, famously described the indeterminate, fragmenting experience of battle as the 'fog of war'.[6] Bowman's sonnets, like those of Sassoon, might be seen as frustrated attempts to condense such fog into fourteen lines of ordered words. Less ostensibly angry and purposeful than Sassoon, Bowman attempts instead to simply explore the chaos through the patterning form of the sonnet. This is well illustrated in Sonnet 7 of the sequence (4), which begins with an observation about the fog of war and a series of questions, beginning 'What of our comrades in the forward post?', before concluding in further questions:

> Ah, stay,
> Pale sergeant. Do you bleed? You came that way?
> What is the tidings? Is the front line lost?
> 'Nothing is known of the posts that lie before
> Laventie. At the cross-roads hellish fire
> Has cut them off who shouldered the first load.'
> Can they live through it? 'They can not retire,

Nor can you reinforce. I know no more
But this. No living thing comes down that road.'

Although Bowman employs the regular rhyme scheme and iambic pentameter of the conventional sonnet here, he also uses techniques like run-on-lines and caesuras to break up the poem's rhythm and give it a sense of confusion. The dialogue of questions and imperfect answers reinforces this, as does the use of colloquial, unpoetic language describing actual, immediate events and not the abstractions and rationalisations we often find in sonnets. The general effect is of a rushed bulletin from the front line and not the meditative rumination or gestural rhetoric we might normally expect of the form.

This mismatching of form and content creates a kind of dissonance in Bowman's battle poems – representing either the failed attempts of an individual to render the chaos of war in comprehensible forms, or an ironic interrogation of the belief that any order at all can come from such bewilderment. In the poems dealing with his experience as a prisoner of war, however, there is arguably a more interesting and penetrating use of the form. In Sonnet 3 of his 'Rastatt' sequence (5), Bowman writes powerfully of his and his fellows' confinement and yearning for freedom:

> Within these cages day by day we pace
> The bitter shortness of the meted span;
> And this and that way variously we plan
> Our poor excursions over the poor place,
> Cribbed to extinction. Yet remains one grace.
> For neither bars nor tented wire can ban
> Full many a roving glance that dares to scan
> The roomy hill, and wanders into space.
> Yea, and remains for every unrepealed
> And unimpaired the free impetuous quest
> Of the mind's soaring eye, at length unsealed

> To the full measure of a life possessed
> Awhile, but never counted, now revealed
> Inestimable, wonderful, unguessed.

Even without considering its form, the poem offers a powerful evocation of freedom seen from captivity and a testament to the power of the imagination in seeking an escape from confinement. Particularly interesting is the way in which the poem uses metaphors of measurement and of vision to develop its wider argument: moving from a 'meted span' and a rather furtive 'roving glance that dares to scan / The roomy hill' boldly as it gathers confidence to 'the mind's soaring eye, at length unsealed / To the full measure of a life'.

But when one considers that it is a sonnet, and especially a Petrarchan sonnet employing only four rhymes in a strictly controlled pattern (abba abba cd cd cd), then it becomes even more remarkable. What better form could there be, one might think, for a work that is struggling to express a vision of ecstatic freedom seen in confinement than one of the most confined and constricting poetic forms of all? And when one reads again the first two lines, with their description of pacing 'these cages day by day' and the 'bitter shortness of the meted span', it is perhaps not too fanciful to suggest that these are descriptions of the poem itself and of the poetic speaker whose ecstatic vision is caged within them. This reading is perhaps reinforced when one remembers that poetic metres are often described as 'measures', that they are 'scanned' into verse, and that poems pace on metrical feet. The placement of such words, 'pace', 'measure', 'scan', then, are perhaps more than coincidental, and make the sonnet a meditation on the tensions present in poetic as well as physical confinement.

Similar, if not quite so ingenious attempts to bend form rather than break it entirely can be seen in the work of several Scottish soldier poets. One interesting example can be found in the work of **Roderick Watson Kerr**, and in particular his poem 'June, 1918' (31). It is clear in the way that the poem is structured, with the second stanza offering a kind of grotesque reworking of the first, that Kerr is highlighting the ways in which the expectations raised in conventional poetry are shaken to their foundations by the experience of war.

The first stanza offers a highly conventional representation of late spring / early summer replete with roses that are 'emblems of heaven', 'blithesome birds', 'cool sweet winds', reveries of 'Palaces in Paradise' and two kissing lovers joyful by 'sun-lit waters'. The language and tone here are those that are expected of poetic reverie. The language is poetic and figurative (only poets talk of 'blithesome birds', or describe emblematic, heavenly roses crooning 'Strange melodies in garden and in hedge', or use contractions such as 'flow'rs' and 'show'rs', or compare the 'incense' drenched on the air by flowers to 'Intoxicating wine'). It is literary, too, inviting the reader to compare the heady experience of spring with the ecstatic visions of Coleridge's poem 'Kubla Khan'. And it reinforces its sense of a universal harmony by employing a regular iambic metre, with ten-syllable five-stress lines, rhymed in couplets.

The impression given by the first stanza is that of an atmosphere found in much romantic poetry after Wordsworth and Keats, in which man and nature co-exist in a benignly harmonious relationship and the job of the poet is to plumb the deep, sacred mysteries of that relationship. The second stanza, it is clear, describes a quite different relationship, and it does this by employing a distinctly different tone. The poem's intention is clearly to shock, by contrasting in a systematic way the cosy assumptions of romantic poetry with the grim realities to which men are exposed in battle. From the first couplet we see the benign poetic imagery of the first stanza turned chaotically on its head, with 'the joyous, sun-filled month of June' transforming in front of our eyes into 'a writhing, war-gorged month of hell'. The organic imagery of the first stanza, epitomised by the sweet rose, is transformed into the cold inorganic imagery of 'steel and iron and high explosive'. The rose's mellifluous 'croon' transmogrifies into a 'yell' and the 'Cursed cacophonies' of the guns, while the homely, reassuring 'garden' and 'hedge' become 'blasted plains'. The songs of 'blithesome birds' become 'singeing bullets singing in the lanes', and the flowers' sweet incense transforms into the poisonous vapours of a gas attack. The poetic ecstasy that in the first stanza takes hold of the mind under the intoxicating influence of the flowers' scent to create 'fair dreams of Palaces in Paradise' turns in the second stanza into a paroxysm altogether more horrific, the gas taking hold of the soldier's body with 'strangling hands that clutch and tear at him'. The final image seals the horror of this transformation, with the innocent lovers kissing in the grass turned into two soldiers clutching each other in a deadly embrace, and the passing 'sun-lit waters' changed into the 'spurting red' of their blood.

In its word choice and imagery this stanza might be said to be half way to modernism in its rejection of the platitudes of romantic nature poetry and its embrace of hard, unpoetic phrasing. But it is interesting to note that the howl and protest of the second stanza's language remains contained in the harmonious form that shapes the first stanza: the poem retains a more or less regular iambic pentameter and couplet rhyme scheme to its end. It might be argued that this enhances the poem's irony, with the final four lines of each stanza ending with the same rhyming words – 'Khan' / 'fan', 'grass' / 'pass' – reinforcing the sense that the second stanza is acting as a kind of gross distorting mirror on the assumptions contained in the first. But it could also be said that Kerr is perhaps resisting the final step towards the kinds of radical disintegration of form found in modernism – that he is either reluctant to push his form past breaking point in order to reflect the war's chaos and confusion, or that he believes that it remains the poet's task to make some kind of order out of that chaos.

Kerr's war poetry did experiment with less rigid verse forms, perhaps most interestingly with a free verse of varying line lengths in the devotional poem 'Faith' (29). In this poem the speaker places his life in God's hands and submits himself to His will, creating a contemplative state of grace through the use of a pared-down simple language. The poem concludes:

> If He should will it,
> He will put a bullet thro' my head;
> Or tear my limbs asunder with a shell;
> Or glean my entrails out;
> Or make me foam and choke with gas:
> And 'twill be well.
>
> But, if He will it,
> He will turn the bullets in their flight;
> Will make a stoppage in a gun;
> Or make a gunner's hand to tremble,
> That his aim be false –
>
> And winds of bullets will cool my cheeks,
> And shrapnel fall like blossoms on my head!

The simplicity is created here by a deliberately unsophisticated language, with whole lines – 'If He should will it', 'Or make me foam and choke with gas', 'That his aim be false' – that are made up of words of one syllable. But lest this be mistaken for the experiments of modernism it is important to notice also how sophisticated and structured the poem is: each line is end-stopped with a punctuation mark, meaning that it must be read slowly, something that is reinforced by the use of anaphora in the repetitions of 'He', 'Or', and 'And' at the beginning of lines. Perhaps the original, and certainly one of the most celebrated, uses of anaphora is in the Biblical Psalms, and it is perhaps here we should look for the principal influence on Kerr's poem. In spite of its unbiblical subject matter of guns and bullets and shells, the poem maintains a biblical register through its simplified language and its use of archaic phrases of punishment, such as 'tear my limbs asunder' and 'glean my entrails out', as well as those of grace, seen especially in the final two lines.

One final poem by Kerr illustrates a slightly different relation to the poetic tradition, this time in undercutting the assumptions of a specific poem. Rupert Brooke's 'Soldier' sonnet, it will be remembered begins with the line 'If I should die, think only this of me' before going on to describe a 'rich earth' sanctified by the 'richer dust' of the English soldier's body placed in it. Kerr plainly had this image and poem in mind when he began his 'Denial' (30):

> If I should die – chatter only this: –
> 'A bullet flew by that did not miss!'
> I did not give life up because of a friend;
> That bullet came thro', and that was the end!
>
> Don't put up a cross where my dung will be laid,
> But scatter some wheat – and bread will be made;
> Don't say I'm a hero because I was shot;
> A bullet won't make one what one is not.
>
> Don't scribble my name upon Honour's scroll
> And plaster it up on the Churches hall:
> What honour is there in being forced to die?
> We slaughter a pig – but we make it a fry!

The 'denial' of which the poem speaks is plainly that of the reassuring sentiments of Brooke's poem. Kerr takes Brooke's central image – of a soldier's body invested in the land – and strips away its sentimental dressing, turning away from Brooke's sanctifying impulses towards something much more profane and banal. This is signalled in the first line, where Brooke's 'think only this of me', with its elevating sentiment and involved syntax, becomes a prosaic and almost dismissive 'chatter only this'. This tone persists in Kerr's speaker's refusal to ascribe a higher motive to his potential sacrifice, denying that he is giving up his life for others, and describing his body – what Brooke had called 'a richer dust' – simply as 'my dung'.

In Brooke's world one would imagine that names might be 'etched' or 'inscribed' on the Roll of Honour, but in Kerr's world they are 'scribbled'. And where Brooke's speaker turns his eyes up to an English heaven Kerr's speaker looks down to the earth, comparing the death of a soldier to the slaughter of a pig (though, as the poem is quick to note, there is at least a purpose and a useful end-product in killing a pig). The sense that it is plainly absurd to ascribe a sense of honour to the random slaughter of war is aptly summarised by the blunt common-sense of Kerr's pithy observation: 'Don't say I'm a hero because I was shot; / A bullet won't make one what one is not'.

LANGUAGE

The simplicity and directness of Kerr's language, even while it works within long-established formal conventions, is itself a kind of challenge to the expectation that serious poetic discussions of life and death demand an elevated diction. As such, his work can be seen as part of a larger movement challenging the way language is characterised in poetry, and in particular the assumption that the only proper medium for serious poetry was the elevated English spoken by the British middle class.

This challenge can be found across a range of the Scottish poetry of the First World War. Perhaps the most obvious instances can be found in the work of Scots Gaelic soldier-poets, like **Dòmhnall Ruadh Chorùna/Donald**

Macdonald (39), **Iain Rothach/John Munro** (57), and **Murchadh Moireach/Murdo Murray** (68). Their poems remind us not simply of the significance of the Gaels in the Highland regiments and their traditions of military service, but that Gaelic itself is a flexible poetic language working hard, like other languages, to adapt itself to the unprecedented conditions of modern war: that Gaelic is not simply a historical language with application only to a limited local landscape and a small indigenous community, but rather an outward-looking world language, capable of reaching out to describe and comprehend the complexities of the world of modernity.

Such issues were also in the minds of those who sought to use the Scots language to encapsulate the experience of war. For a long time Scots had, in literary and social terms, been treated as something of a subordinate language: a language appropriate for couthy comedy and homely sentiment but not for rational argument or professional discourse. The Scottish education system of the late nineteenth-century proved itself an efficient machine for turning out people who understood that effective communication depended not just on what one said, but on how one said it. The successes of that system were adept code-switchers, knowing well that English was the proper language to use in one's dealings with authority and officialdom while Scots might remain a good, rooted domestic language for relating to one's more intimate and informal networks. The failures of this system were those who were stuck in Scots, who, it was assumed, were unable to communicate effectively with their social and educational betters and were thus condemned to a limited, parochial understanding of the wider world.

The first wholly sustained challenge to these assumptions, and the first significant attempts to create a parity of status between English and Scots as literary languages, would come after the First World War through the work of Hugh MacDiarmid and the Scottish Literary Renaissance. But there were several stirrings during the war that suggested that writers were finding their own way towards such a realisation. The most significant of these were the writers of the Doric revival in North East Scotland, but others like the Dundee poet **Joseph Lee** can be seen exploring ways in which Scots-language poetry might branch out beyond the limiting kinds of conventional comedy or the sentimentality that we have already seen in the work of Mackenzie MacBride and Charles Murray.

Lee was an unashamedly popular poet, influenced by both Robert Burns and Rudyard Kipling, and like many popular pre-war Scottish poets had a tendency to employ literary English for his more serious, philosophical and didactic poems and dialect Scots for his humorous historical and observational poems – a mixture seen in his 1910 collection *Poems: Tales o' our Town*. In the poetry he wrote as a soldier and as a prisoner of war this did not change enormously – if anything his work moves away from Burns's Scots to Kipling's Cockney – but occasionally, in poems such as 'The Carrion Crow' (34), it is possible to see him experimenting with Scots as a means of exploring some of the more sinister implications of war.

It might be said that the use of Scots in the poem invokes folk traditions of supernaturalism, so that Lee is merely continuing to use the language to depict a limited range of experience and a form of native credulousness. The poem certainly picks up on the traditional Scottish ballad 'The Twa Corbies', in which two crows discourse on the prospect of glutting themselves on the body of a dead knight: Lee's poem is, like 'The Twa Corbies', formed in couplets of iambic tetrameter; his use of the archaic word 'wot' (to know) is perhaps a direct reference to the lines in 'The Twa Corbies', 'In behint yon auld fail dyke / I wot there lies a new-slain knight'; and his crow's threat that 'I'll pike out baith thy bonnie een' repeats that of the corbie in the earlier poem, that 'I'll pike out his bonny blue een'.

But the poem also draws on a broader tradition of gothic literature that allows it also to be seen in a wider context. A comparison might be made with Edgar Allan Poe's poem 'The Raven' (1845), whose speaker also enters into a dialogue with a portentous black bird. Like Lee's poem, and unlike 'The Twa Corbies', Poe's poem focuses on the human narrator rather than the bird itself. Lee's crow is more eloquent than Poe's raven (which restricts itself to one word, 'Nevermore') but in the case of both poems it's arguable that the dialogue with what Poe describes as his 'Ghastly grim and ancient raven' and Lee a 'horrid, hooded, hoary crow' is a manifestation of a profound inner disturbance on the part of the speaker. As such, the poem offers much more than a simple sinister or supernatural encounter, becoming instead a probing exploration of a troubled psychological condition.

The First World War, and in particular his experience of treating patients with war trauma, caused Sigmund Freud to revise his model of the unconscious mind and incorporate within it what he described as the *Todestrieb*, or 'death drive'. Recognising, in his essay 'Beyond the Pleasure Principle' (1920), the compulsion in the human mind to return to and repeat traumatic experiences, he posited the presence of a drive that counterbalanced and occasionally overwhelmed what he had previously assumed were our natural instincts towards pleasure and self-gratification.[7] It would probably be going too far to describe Lee's poem as a manifestation of this specific Freudian idea, but it is perhaps interesting to see the correspondences, witnessed particularly in the speaker's compulsive fascination with this bird and the way he turns it into a repetitive dialogue speculating on his own death: repeating words like 'pike' ('I'll pike out baith thy bonnie een; / I'll pike the flesh frae off each bane'); and reworking the opening three stanzas into the poem's final three stanzas (making the poem sound reiterative and circular, and so quite unlike the linearity of the ballad narrative of 'The Twa Corbies').

What is also particularly interesting, given the comparison with Freud, is the way Lee's speaker associates death with a contorted form of sexuality. There is something more than just straightforward description going on in the crow's assertion that it will repeatedly 'pike' the speaker's dead body with the whetted blade of its beak, and the uneasiness continues into the next couplet in which the act of pecking bare the speaker's face is likened grotesquely to the kiss of a lover. Here the direct, unadorned dialect voice brings not just a grimness and immediacy that would be much more difficult to achieve in a conventional poetic voice, but it also allows a potentially sophisticated insight into the strange relationship between sex and death: between what Freud characterised as the *Eros* associated with love, life, and procreation and the *Thanatos* that pushes us unconsciously towards death, compulsive repetition, and self-destruction.

THE HOME FRONT

It would be a mistake to assume that all war poetry is written by active combatants. As we have already seen in the poetry written before hostilities had properly begun, the anticipation, experience, and consequences of the war had an impact that spread far wider than the battlefield or immediate theatre of war itself. This was hardly new. Von Clausewitz had recognised that war was not an isolated phenomenon but was in fact rooted deeply in social experience, stating in a famous phrase that 'war is the continuation of politics by other means'. What was new in the twentieth century was the concept of Total War that would characterise the First and, even more so, the Second World Wars: a recognition that wars were no longer being fought by representative armies, as at Waterloo or Balaclava, but by whole populations. The notion of the 'home front' was the invention of the First World War as it became realised that civilian populations were fundamental components of the national war effort, so that engineers and ship-builders, miners, munitions workers, civil servants, farmers, nurses, home-economists and home-makers all came to be seen as important components in a national war machine.

In such circumstances those who weren't in uniform had as much of a concern about the war and its effects as those who were; they might be in less immediate danger of their lives but they had as much to win or lose from the war in the longer term as those actively engaged in the fighting. And this concern was reflected in the poetry that was written by non-combatants throughout the war. In the war's first phase, much of this poetry expressed – as we have seen – a broad enthusiasm for war, consisting of prideful accounts of national history and character and expressions of a resolution to defeat what was seen as continental tyranny. This enthusiasm prompted a glut of poetic submissions to newspapers and journals across the UK, to the point that some imposed a moratorium, pleading with their readers to stop sending unsolicited poems. The Glasgow entertainments paper *The Bailie* commented humorously on this glut in October 1914, noting that in the present circumstances 'everyone seems to be hammering out verse to the best of his, her, or its ability'.

The early hopes of a swift victory proved misguided, however, and as the war fell into a slow, agonised routine much civilian poetry turned from active enthusiasm to more indirect forms of keeping up morale. This can be seen in the poetry published by women in Scottish factory journals such as the *Cardonald News* and *Georgetown Gazette*, which seemed mainly concerned, like the trench journals produced by soldiers, with broadly good-humoured comment on the new conditions, and sometime absurdities, thrown up by the war. 'A Whiff o' Hame' by **Mary Symon** (84) captures something of this spirit of cheerfully wilful morale-boosting. Written as the introduction to a Christmas book that was sent out to soldiers in 1916, Symon offers a light, sentimental reassurance that they are not forgotten, and that just as they think fondly of their homeland their homeland is thinking 'Wi' love and pride o' you, lads'. From a 'norland river' to 'the mists abeen Loch Lomond, / An' the stars owre Benachie', Symon evokes a geographically diverse national landscape – a 'whiff o' hame' – that is used to sustain those who find themselves temporarily exiled from it. And like Mackenzie MacBride, she invokes a sentimental pride to turn this landscape and all its associations into a kind of *casus belli*, a justification for war based on the defence of its values, having her soldiers cry at the conclusion to the poem, '"The old Land's worth it – / Dear God, it's worth it a'!"'

Some poetry by non-combatants, however, took a more sombre view of the absurdity of war and its purported defence of home. This was the case of the poems of **John MacDougall Hay**, a minister of religion and author of the novel *Gillespie* (1914). His poem, 'The Call' (22) is, like Watson Kerr's 'Denial', an attempt to strip war of any glamorous trappings in which militarists might want to dress it. MacDougall Hay employs a form that owes much to the King James Bible, with verses of irregular length and freedom from rhyme, to remind us that, as the poem puts it, that soldiers 'did not put off humanity when they put on a uniform'. The soldiers he describes are not moved by 'Military pomp, pride, pageantry and gorgeousness of arms' but instead by an impulse rooted more firmly in their domestic ground. The heroism they embody is not that of aggression and conquest, but a more patient Christian one of suffering on behalf of those they love:

> Do not think of them as soldiers as they pass by, the
>   companions of horses, living among steel and
>   explosives.
> They were men like you.
> They had their own burdens, anxieties and cares;
> A mother to support; children the leaving of whom behind
>   was the first death.

> To none is home dearer than to those who go forth to fight
> for home.

MacDougall Hay's poem is a reminder that while war might sometimes be seen as an abstract, distant activity fought by remote armies it is always grounded in the experience of people just like us, people who suffered 'heavy thoughts' and 'had bad news in letters, and cried at night in their dug-out or billet'. His poetry, in this way, might be said to bring the war home to the reader – to remind us that this is a war that is being fought by civilians, even if they happen to be wearing uniforms for the duration.

A rather different and rather less elevated take on the home front can be found in 'Dockens Afore his Peers' by **Charles Murray** (64). Murray's poem takes the form of a dramatic monologue, a form that Robert Browning had done much to advance in the nineteenth century in which a speaker reveals himself and his world gradually to the reader, eventually giving more of himself away than perhaps he realises. Browning's most celebrated poems in this form include 'My Last Duchess' and 'Fra Lippo Lippi' and both are masterpieces of self-incrimination, showing us in the first the frightening vanity and malignity lying just beneath the surface of a powerful, urbane man of affairs, and in the second the roguish charm of a painter in holy orders whose inspiration comes less from the spirit than from his observations of earthy, venal life and the pleasures of the opposite sex.

Murray's poem is more overtly comical than Browning's monologues, dealing as it does with power at a less elevated level. Where Browning tended towards using a blank verse form consisting of unrhymed lines of iambic pentameter, Murray employs a kind of variation of ballad form similar to that which we have noted in Kipling and in Campbell, consisting of a fourteen-syllable line in rhymed couplets with each line having a break between an eight-syllable first part and six-syllable second. The rhymes arguably assist the comedy, making the speaker's glibness more apparent and the poem's resolution more pat.

The poem's speaker is John Watt, the prosperous, somewhat bumptious farmer of Dockenhill, and the poem consists of his garrulous but sly testimony to a local Enlistment Exemption Tribunal. Dockenhill is clearly well-known to the members of the board (signalled by the use of the familiar diminutive 'Dockens' in the title) and affects to treating the matter lightly as just one of the many small tasks that bring him into town that morning. He chats blithely about the weather and his business with the saddler and the clockmaker, the banker's wife and the farrier, taking a pinch of snuff from a familiar on the tribunal along the way and assuring them they shouldn't really waste too much time and effort over this: 'Ye winna hinner lang wi' me, an' speer a lot o' buff'. All he needs, he says, is 'a line / To say there's men that maun be left, an' ye've exemptit mine'. When challenged that he has people enough to work his farm he launches into a long list of the qualities of his employees and his family: from his doughty, thrifty wife; his delicate, musical daughter freshly returned from boarding school; the 'kitchie deem' or maid who appears to do all the real work in the house and whom he admits would make the best soldier if it weren't for her gender ('Gie her a kilt instead o' cotts, an' thon's the gran' recruit'); through all the workers on his farm from his elderly grieve Francie and his two incompetent ploughmen to the poor soul who acts as his stuttering, club-footed baillie. Dockenhill's account of a dysfunctional workforce is comic and self-serving, and the reader learns much that is both amusing and alarming about the complacency and the canniness traditionally ascribed to successful Aberdeenshire farmers.

The poem culminates in his arguments on behalf of the final member of the household, his son Johnnie who is plainly the most obvious potential recruit. Dockenhill explores every angle in arguing against his son's enlistment: first of all omitting to mention him until the tribunal notices him waiting in the gig; then attempting to claim he's too young ('he's a littlan jist, for a' he leuks sae big'); then that he'd be too scared and, besides, that they have plans to send him to town to train him as a land-surveyor and, in a final appeal to pity, that "Twould kill his mither, that, / To think o' Johnnie in a trench awa in fat-ye-ca't'. As Dockenhill starts to run out of arguments he suggests they take any of the others instead – wife, daughter, maid, grieve, ploughmen, baillie – before weakening his son's case even further by listing the indispensable tasks he takes in the work of the farm. These comprise the hardly overwhelming jobs of digging the yard, scything weeds, wisping straw, sitting with his father and taking notes at cattle sales, tidying the desk, taking a hand at cards and driving his father home when he's drunk. Just as his son's case seems lost, however, Dockenhill plays his final and decisive card, reminding three members of the tribunal of their personal and financial debts to him:

> Hoot, Mains, hae mind, I'm doon for you some sma' thing
>   wi' the bank;
> Aul' Larickleys, I saw you throu', an' this is a' my thank;
> An' Gutteryloan, that time ye broke, to Dockenhill ye cam' –
> 'Total Exemption.' Thank ye, sirs. Fat say ye till a dram?

The abruptness of the conclusion is an apt reminder of what Dockenhill had said at the beginning of his testimony, that they might have saved themselves a lot of effort if they had simply given him what he wanted in the first place. His blustering attempts at charm, his self-important, man-of-affairs attitude, and his wily arguments are all trumped by the mundane fact that he has all these members of a small, interlinked community in his pocket. There is perhaps little of the philosophical subtlety found in Browning's dramatic monologues here, but there is still something unwholesome and corrupt that creeps out beneath the broad Doric comedy. It is difficult to know whether contemporary readers of the poem would have been amused or outraged by the poem; whether they were entertained by a fresh and cleverly framed insight into the stock figure of the canny, prosperous farmer or were instead appalled at the cynicism that allows the wealthy and well-connected to avoid their duty. Perhaps, like many good poems, it made (and makes) readers feel both at the same time. What is certain is that it shows a Doric language capable of demonstrating the complex psychological and social issues that lie submerged beneath the beguiling surface of its comedy.

MEMORY

The kinds of comedy and high rhetoric found in the work of Murray and MacDougall Hay have little place in the significant body of poetry, by both combatants and non-combatants, that dealt with the longer lasting personal effects of war: particularly the memory of trauma and of the personal loss of loved ones in the conflict. Several of the most moving of these poems were written by women who experienced that loss in its rawest form through the deaths of their children.

Before we get to these, however, it is first worth focusing on a poem that deals with a similar experience of loss from the soldier's viewpoint. **E. A. Mackintosh's** 'In Memoriam' (47) is the speaker's attempt, as its subtitle tells us, to come to terms with the death of Private David Sutherland, who died under Mackintosh's command during a trench raid near Arras in May 1916. 'In Memoriam' begins as a second-person address to Sutherland's father and, like several poems we have already looked at, draws on the evocative power of parental grief – particularly in its depiction of the bereaved father as 'an old man weeping, / Just an old man in pain'. What takes this image beyond the kind of conventional pathos we have seen in similar images in the work of Cameron and Cocker is the detail with which Mackintosh invests it: the way he delineates the relationship between a boy who saves his father's feelings by writing to him only of the seasons and the farming year and not the awful realities of war, and the corresponding details of the farmwork that will now be left undone because of a disabling grief.

As the poem develops, however, its subject shifts and its tone moves from consolation towards something closer to despair. This is signalled in the rather unexpected phrase that begins the third stanza, 'You were only David's father, but I had fifty sons', which has the effect of shifting the burden of bereavement away from Sutherland's father onto the speaker, Mackintosh, himself. The word 'only' might be seen to be slighting or disrespectful here, and the poem undoubtedly risks offending conventional sentiment in its suggestion that the comradeship of arms is stronger than the bonds of family. Mackintosh, it must be remembered, had only recently turned twenty-three, when he wrote this, and to state baldly, as he does, that his men were 'More my sons' than their fathers' might seem presumptuous. But the poem arguably makes good on this claim through its depiction of the deeper trust that is brought about by the sharing of experiences that turn 'beautiful men' into 'piteous writhing bodies'. It is one thing, the poem suggests, to bring a new being into the world and protect and succour it, but quite another to hold and try vainly to console it as it is torn from existence in pain and anguish.

'In Memoriam' begins by apostrophising a particular father in the second-person singular as 'you' but ends by addressing fathers generally in the third-person plural as them – 'they could only see / The little helpless babies', 'they were only your fathers'. The 'you' of the last two stanzas of the poem has become the second-person plural of the soldiers themselves

– 'never will I forget you, / My men that trusted me', 'they could not see you dying'. The revaluation of paternity and paternal roles seen here is more than a matter of grammar, for it speaks to a wider sense that developed among many soldiers of a distrust of conventional authority figures – those whom Samuel Hynes called the 'old men at home who had lied to them',[8] and who Mackintosh described in 'Recruiting' (49) as 'the fat old men' who take credit for the victories of the young soldiers. 'In Memoriam' does not so much confront that generation as gently supplant it. Mackintosh remains sympathetic to the pain felt by Sutherland's father, but attempts to show the ways in which the terrible, accelerated experiences of war might instil in a junior officer in his early twenties a more profound grief over the death of a young man than that found even in his natural father.

Such an overturning of conventional paternal authority is felt too in the rhyme. The only imperfect rhymes in the whole poem are those that complete stanza two and the poem's concluding stanza, and which deal with its most important word, 'officer'. It is perhaps no casual error that this most definite word in the military hierarchy here loses much of its power through its operation as a weak half-rhyme (stormier / officer; 'Don't leave me, Sir' / officer). Mackintosh is perhaps telling us indirectly that the man who wears an officer's uniform is not so much the fixed and definite authority on which the military insists and on which it depends for its stability, as a fallible fellow-sufferer, as insecure and uncertain as the rest of humankind.

Such views, however, cannot take away from the depths of suffering experienced by parents, and especially that of bereaved mothers and wives who could have no sense of control or agency over the terrible, distant events of the war. Mackintosh has, at least, an outlet for his sorrow in anger and action, but most women had no such opportunities and were condemned instead to grieve their losses in awful passivity.

Violet Jacob was already established as a significant figure in the Doric revival when she learned that her son Harry had been killed in the Battle of the Somme. Two of the poems that come out of that experience, 'The Field by the Lirk o' the Hill' (24) and 'The Road to Marykirk' (25) express her sense of loss in different ways. 'The Field by the Lirk o' the Hill' is, like 'Dockens afore his Peers', written in the rich Doric of Scotland's north-east. But there is a strong contrast between Murray's garrulous tone and the terse, tight-lipped economy of Jacob's language. Jacob's speaker begins, like Dockenhill, with observations on the weather, but to a very different purpose:

Daytime an' nicht,
   Sun, wind an' rain
The lang, cauld licht
   O' the spring months again.

The shorter line lengths here contrast with the sprawl of Murray's, suggesting a greater economy of emotion, and where Dockenhill's observations on the weather are part of his bustling, businesslike approach to getting things done in his own way, here there is a suggestion of almost mute resignation to the relentless progress of the days and the seasons. The absence of a verb in this first sentence amplifies the sense in which the speaker is made to seem passive and helpless in the face of external events. The frigidity of the imagery and the language, and the predominant use of simple, one-syllable words – a contrast to the garrulousness of Murray's Dockenhill – suggest a mind turning in on itself, refusing expansiveness and speculation. The reason becomes clear when the addressee of the poem becomes apparent: the 'ye' who the poem talks to in its second stanza is dead and so will be forever absent from the landscape, 'the field by the lirk o' the hill', that is being described. There is no response to the shrill cry of the 'whaups', the curlews that haunt moorland and shoreline, other than a blank realisation of absence: 'An' you nae mair'.

This sense in which nature is oblivious to the deaths of countrymen (made mordantly by Charles Hamilton Sorley in 'All the Hills and Vales Along') is again present in 'The Road to Marykirk'. This is a less immediately sombre poem than 'The Field by the Lirk o' the Hill', offering in its first stanza a lively account of travelling on the road to Marykirk in the shadow of the Grampians. The longer line length, with regular iambic tetrameters and an abab rhyme, create a sense of life and movement, signalled by the first line: 'To Marykirk ye'll set ye forth, / An' whustle as ye step alang'. The ominous whaups of 'The Field by the Lirk o' the Hill' are replaced by more sociable lapwings: 'teuchits, skirlin' on the wing'. But this sense of movement is arrested in the poem's final two lines, in which, the harsh realisation comes home to the speaker that all this life can mean nothing to her dead 'Jock' who lies dead in Flanders. Both poems attempt to elicit the reader's sympathy by using apostrophe – directly addressing a dead loved-one in the second person 'you' – but while the first poem creates a sense of emotional devastation through an affectless monotone, the second attempts to show a similar devastation by the use of contrast: offering instead of numbness in the face of nature an appalled realisation that every life-giving blast of nature 'blaws a thocht to mock / The licht o' day on ilka thing'.

Although 'The Road to Marykirk' suggests that there is little consolation in nature, it does at least register the beauty of the natural landscape and try to make some connection between that landscape and the soldier who, by implication, died in order to preserve it. For many writers dealing with the war's terrible aftermath, and for those who set about building memorials to it, such associations became increasingly consoling and important. Many writers found themselves adopting the literary form of pastoral elegy as an appropriate way of memorialising the sacrifice made by servicemen in the defence of their country. A classical form that had been brought into the English-language tradition by poems such as Milton's 'Lycidas', Shelley's 'Adonaïs', and Arnold's 'Thyrsis', pastoral elegy is a way of remembering a dead person through the memories they leave in the countryside they have inhabited. This became especially important in the First World War, given the decree that no bodies of those who died fighting abroad were to be repatriated for burial in the United Kingdom. With no grave on which mourning could focus, many sought to use the landscape itself as a memorial, and used poetry as a form of consoling themselves that the dead somehow lived on in the spirit of particular places.

This convention applied also to the building of physical memorials in rural areas, the majority of which were not built in centres of population but in local scenic beauty spots with prospects of hills, green spaces, or the sea. These can still be seen on hillsides and shorelines all over rural Scotland; perhaps the best-known fictional example is the war memorial that is built above Kinraddie in Lewis Grassic Gibbon's *Sunset Song* (1932), the consecration of which supplies the novel with its wonderfully melancholic lament for the passing of the old Scottish ways.

'The Soldiers' Cairn' by **Mary Symon** (80), uses both the idea of pastoral elegy and of rural memorialisation to create another moving portrayal of loss and bereavement. As in pastoral elegy, the speaker of the poem assumes that the most fitting place in which the dead should be remembered is the landscape above the town, in which they played as children:

> Gie me a hill wi' the heather on't,
>   And a reid sun drappin' doon,
> Or the mists o' the mornin' risin' saft
>   Wi' the reek owre a wee grey toon.

She tells of a child's fishing rod still hanging on a willow, an 'aul' sauch tree', while its owner lies dead in Picardy, and of a boy's name whittled into an alder that will now be seen carved in the stone of the soldiers' cairn. Her account closes with a hope and with a fear. The hope is that the sacrifice of the soldiers has not been worthless, and that it will somehow come to epitomise 'the Dream Divine of a starward way' and render their memorial 'a new earth's corner-stone'. The fear, that the community's gesture of remembrance may not live up to the sacrifice it attempts to commemorate: that 'This lanely cairn on a hameland hill / Is a' that oor love can dee'. This fearful note is reinforced in the poem's conclusion: a cry of irreparable loss from the maternal heart, that speaks more of desolation than consolation,

> *But oh, my Bairn, my Bairn,*
> *It's a cradle's croon that'll aye blaw doon*
> *To me fae the Soldiers' Cairn.*

But, of course, the poem itself is a kind of memorial in words to the dead, a fact that is reinforced by the speaker herself when she says that 'it's nae wi' stane or airn [iron], / But wi' brakin' herts, and mem'ries sair / That we're biggin' [building] the Soldiers' Cairn'. The suggestion here is that the Soldiers' Cairn is not just the physical object being described but the poem itself; the words piled up on the page as we read them. To read the poem, then, might itself be thought of as an act of remembrance and a means of allaying its speaker's fears: its words are more articulate than the mute stone of the cairn and allow for the expression of just those emotions that she fears can never be expressed by a conventional memorial.

It's important to note something else that this poem does that sets it apart from much of the official memorialisation of the war: it remembers the dead in their own dialect and something like their own voice, speaking of the places they loved in a language they would recognise and use. This is something that happens rarely in official memorials of the First World War, which tend towards a register and a vocabulary that comes from a more elevated, more formal, and therefore perhaps rather more alien discourse. As Symon's speaker says, memorials are built out of memories as much as they are built out of stone. By building her memorial in words, she is able not only to give voice to that memory and make it last as long as those words are read, but to do so in a way that speaks more directly, and perhaps truly, of the lives and experiences it commemorates.

THE SECOND WORLD WAR: 1939–1945

'THIS WAR, LIKE THE NEXT WAR,
IS A WAR TO END WAR.'

– *Attributed to David Lloyd George, 1916*

There is an enormous social and political gulf between the societies of 1914 and 1939. The aftermath of any war and its impact on society is as much a part of the story of conflict as the actual fighting. This was never truer than in the years after 1918. One way or another, the cost of winning the 'war to end wars' had changed everything. The Great War had been a brutal education for many of those who survived, often physically damaged, emotionally traumatised, or deeply disaffected. Writing in the 1920s Ernest Hemingway and William Faulkner imagined a 'lost generation' of young adults in the post-war years, seeking pleasure or distraction in the face of their disillusionment. At a more political level, working-class civilians and soldiers alike had come to see more clearly, perhaps, the true conditions of their common existence in a society rife with inequalities that called on concepts of 'loyalty' and 'duty' to shore itself up, only to fail them when they came home. Old certainties were lost and indeed the map was changing too, for national boundaries around the world were being re-drawn under new priorities and post-war settlements. In particular the experience of economic collapse and the harsh demands imposed on a defeated Germany by the Treaty of Versailles were to pave the way for the rise of fascism in the next generation. As if to add insult to injury, no sooner had fighting ceased than a particularly virulent outbreak of influenza in 1918–19 created a global pandemic that actually killed more people than the war did.

Britain paid a high price for peace, and victory was followed by an economic depression exacerbated by a sharp decline in industrial demand and the deaths of so many servicemen. When a crisis in the American stock exchange in 1929 heralded the Great Depression of the 1930s those effects were felt throughout the Western world. The old industrial centres of Britain, which had been worked to the bone by the demands of the Great War, were particularly hard hit. In the mining and ship-building towns of Scotland, Wales, Northern Ireland and the North of England, for example, almost seventy per cent of working men lost their jobs. This was a time of great hardship, with mass demonstrations, clashes with the police and a succession of hunger marches on the capital. It is one of the terrible ironies of the times that British industry did not really pick up again until the declaration of another war in 1939.

Many socialists in the 1930s saw the Great War, and now the threat of a second conflict, as no more than the struggle for economic and industrial supremacy between rival imperial powers, each intent on commanding the seas and exploiting the wealth of their holdings in Europe, Africa and India. This was certainly the opinion of Sorley MacLean, Scotland's finest Gaelic poet. Nor was he alone in this, for it was the English poet Cecil Day Lewis, also a socialist, who caught something of the spirit of 1939 in his poem 'Where Are the War Poets?' He believed that the capitalist system had 'enslaved religion, market, laws' and now, with the threat of another conflict, writers were being asked to speak up once again for king and country. Day Lewis reflects wearily that it is no more than 'the logic of our times' that poets 'who lived by honest dreams' should be pressed to 'Defend the bad against the worse.'[9]

It is almost impossible for us to imagine what it must have been like to be called to face yet another global conflict, to be fought all over again, within a single person's living memory. Naomi Mitchison was to comment 'Two wars in a lifetime. It seemed unfair. Such a short time since 1918.'[10] Few people doubted, in the end, that the rise of fascism in Germany and

Italy during the 1930s would have to be resisted by those in Europe who still valued democracy, not to mention the clear need to defeat the evil of Hitler's plans for a thousand year Reich based on theories of racial superiority and genocide. Conflict seemed inescapable after the German invasion of Poland in September 1939, but even so, there was little appetite for another World War.

This reluctance was shared by a number of writers and thinkers in Scotland, motivated by both socialist and nationalist sympathies. The Scottish Literary Renaissance of the 1920s had countered the depressing post-war years with a revival of creative confidence in Scottish identity, a new respect for the Scots and Gaelic languages, and a growing sense that a remote government in London had little care for the economic and social problems north of the Border. Writers such as Hugh MacDiarmid, Neil Gunn, Naomi Mitchison and Lewis Grassic Gibbon had claimed new and exciting territory for modern Scottish literature in the twenties and thirties and indeed Grassic Gibbon's *Scots Quair* trilogy describes the social tensions and challenges of exactly that period. (*Sunset Song* can be seen as one of the most moving books about the actual impact of the First World War, and in this respect it makes an unlikely but fascinating companion piece to Virginia Woolf's 1925 novel *Mrs Dalloway*.) For many writers, the Scottish Literary Renaissance had a political dimension too, so that on the outbreak of war, poet and classicist Douglas Young, who was chairman of the Scottish National party at the time, went to court to challenge the British government's legal right to enforce universal conscription in Scotland. It was something of a lost cause from the start, and he served two spells in prison for his efforts. He was not alone, however, for George Campbell Hay resisted conscription for similar reasons. The poet Norman MacCaig's deeply pacifist principles led him to refuse to help the war effort in any way whatsoever, so he served time in prison, even as a conscientious objector.

The novelist Robin Jenkins was another conscientious objector and his novels *The Cone-Gatherers* (1955) and *Guests of War* (1956) derive from his own wartime experiences. The poet Edwin Morgan considered conscientious objection, too, but chose in the end to serve in the RAMC, as what he called 'a sort of pacifist in uniform, in a sense.'[11]

Conscientious objectors could put their case to a tribunal, and, if their case was accepted, they could be granted full exemption, or they might be required to serve in a non-military role such as working on the land, or they might choose to serve as a non-combatant in the army, or in the Royal Army Medical Corps. In contrast to the Great War, universal conscription in Britain was implemented the moment war broke out, which meant that all men from the ages of eighteen to forty-one were liable to serve, except for those on 'reserved occupations' considered vital for the war effort. By 1942 the upper age limit for men was raised to fifty-one, and conscription towards the war effort was introduced for all single women from twenty to thirty years old.

Society had changed a lot since 1914, however, and the conscript armies of 1939 were much better educated than those of any previous generation. Penguin Books had revolutionised publishing in the mid 1930s with their inexpensive paperbacks, and they were swiftly recruited to the war effort by providing quality fiction for an Armed Forces Book Club, as well as guides to philosophy, and culture, not to mention practical guidebooks of all sorts from 'Why Freedom Matters' to growing your own vegetables and identifying enemy aircraft. When Hamish Henderson first arrived in Cairo, he found a thriving literary scene in the armed forces there, publishing magazines with names such as *Citadel* and *Oasis*. In fact one of those army poets and editors, Victor Selwyn, went on to found the Salamander Oasis trust after the war, to collect, preserve and publish the literary efforts of hundreds of servicemen from every theatre of war.

Henderson was not alone as a Scottish poet in North Africa, for Scottish regiments played a key part in that campaign, and at different times, in different locations, G. S. Fraser, Sorley MacLean, George Campbell Hay, Robert Garioch and Edwin Morgan all served in the North African theatre. These poets were not officers, but they were as well or better educated than the officer class of the First War had been. Most of them already thought of themselves as writers and were fully aware of the changes in poetic style and technique that had taken place in the twenties and thirties. Modernism had brought about the acceptance of free verse in the 1920s, often with an experimental bias or a questing intellectual focus and much less emphasis on regular rhyme and metre. Technically and conceptually, the modernist art of the time saw contemporary life as a psychologically and culturally fragmented experience. Thus T. S. Eliot's great poem *The Waste Land* from 1922 was a pessimistic meditation on spiritual desolation, expressed in complex and fragmented images. By the 1930s, however, British poetry was taking a more robust line. Writers such as Stephen Spender, Cecil Day-Lewis, W. H. Auden, Louis MacNeice and Hugh MacDiarmid were marked by a willingness to engage with a satirical or political vision, usually socialist, and a determination to deal with and reflect the problems of modern society and daily life as it was to be found, not in the ruins of traditional culture, or in some idealised English or Scottish countryside, but in the nation's cities and factories. Poetry was changing again.

TOTAL WAR

The nature of modern war was changing too, as those who survived the industrial slaughter in the trenches knew only too well. The Great War had seen Zeppelin raids on London, passenger liners torpedoed, and thousands of women recruited to make shells in the nation's factories. But the post-war years saw much darker changes, with the developing theory of 'total war', which came to regard factories and merchant ships and railways at home, and the civilian population who maintained them, as primary and entirely legitimate targets for direct attack, most especially by increasingly effective aerial bombardment. After all, such resources are instrumental, are they not, in supplying a nation's armies at the front, however remote the actual field of battle might be?

Total war put everyone on the front line and this was certainly the plan for 1939, with the immediate conscription of civilians to join the army, and the recruitment of women to make guns and planes, to work as anti-aircraft spotters, or as 'land girls' on the farms and 'lumber-Jills' in the forests. It is ironic that this was in fact a kind of emancipation for women, as it had been in the First World War (despite the threat to their health in the factories), and many resented the return to peacetime chores and roles when the men came back from fighting. In the early years of the second war, after the experience of the trenches in the first, it was widely feared that poison gas would be used against civilian populations, and so the moment hostilities were declared plans were made to evacuate city children to the relative safety of the countryside, and millions of gasmasks were supplied to every adult, child and baby in the land. Wardens were assigned to be sure that masks were carried at all times, and a major propaganda industry went into action with posters and newsreels to encourage compliance, followed by the building of bombshelters, the rationing of food and clothes, and the issue of identity cards. Everyone was in the army now.

Ironically, the planning needed to maximise the nation's resources and the comprehensive focus required to recruit the masses to the cause of what has since been called 'the people's war' led to full employment, new expectations and new ways of doing things, and this in turn generated a kind of democratic expansion that saw the progressive education act of 1944, and a Labour government elected in 1945, followed by the foundation of the National Health Service by Aneurin Bevan in 1948. But it was not an easy road, and years of food rationing, austerity and industrial recovery were to follow. The logic of total war had led to air raids on London, Birmingham, Coventry, Belfast and Glasgow and eventually to the terrible retaliation of the area bombing of city after city in Germany when early plans for strategic targeting gave way to the easier aims of maximum destruction across the board. The deterrent effect of 'Mutually Assured Destruction' in the post-war nuclear age of the 1960s owed its force to the terrible proof from wartime Europe and the use of atomic bombs to end the Pacific war against Japan, that modern nations in conflict were actually willing to obliterate whole cities of ordinary people in the blink of an eye. We are fortunate (and may never know how fortunate) to have avoided nuclear extinction during the Cold War years, so the Second World War may yet turn out to have been the first and last true example of total war on a global scale. At least we can hope so. This is not to say that the many conflicts of subsequent years have not been equally bloody on a smaller scale, but the human losses of 1939 to 1945 remain uniquely terrible, with combatant and non-combatant fatalities around the world estimated to be somewhere between fifty million and eighty million deaths.

For thousands of people at home in Britain, the front line was now on their doorstep, and this is reflected in many of the poems from that time. It is appropriate that this survey of Scottish poetry from the Second World War should begin with the home front and, most especially, with the experience of women.

THE HOME FRONT

German air raids on RAF stations during the summer of 1940 were intended to clear the skies in advance of Hitler's plans for the invasion of Britain. The RAF managed to hold out, however, with the help of hundreds of observers and plotters all around the south coast and what became known as 'the Battle of Britain' fought by pilots in their Spitfires and Hurricanes has stirred the national imagination ever since. There is an undoubted romance to these 'knights of the air', and in the late 1980s the young Scottish poets Kathleen Jamie and Andrew Greig were inspired to write *A Flame in Your Heart*, a book-length poem sequence about the tragic love affair between a fighter pilot and a nurse during these dangerous summer months. The stressful reality took a heavy toll however, as the Scots poet and airman **Edward Boyd** reminds us when he writes of 'Sir Lancelot in the gutter sprawled, / fish-mouthed and opaque-eyed with alcohol' – 'Visibility Zero' (93). As the year drew on and the opportunities for invasion were diminishing, the German air force began a sustained bombing campaign against Britain's cities and industrial centres. (After the defeat of Dunkirk, while its armies re-formed at home, Britain had sent its own bombers to Berlin as a way of carrying the war to Germany and now the Germans determined to follow suit.)

In the first three weeks of September 1940 the Luftwaffe dropped over five thousand tons of bombs to begin the Blitz on London (the word comes from the German *Blitzkrieg*, meaning 'lightning war'). A nationwide blackout was imposed at night so that the bombers could not see the streets below them, and air raid sirens gave warning of an attack so that people could take cover. Bomb shelters were set up in the streets, or in basements, people's back gardens, or under special steel tables in the house, or even just under the stairs. Barrage balloons, searchlights and anti-aircraft guns were used to hinder the bombers, and people remembered the strange and terrible beauty of these night raids, or so it seemed at least, until dawn revealed the horror of smashed streets and the smoking ruins of demolished houses. Early theorists of aerial bombing had assumed that under the stress of such attacks, civilian morale would crumble and enemy governments would soon be forced to negotiate or surrender. They were wrong. It turned out that civilian populations on both sides were more resilient than expected, and were actually made more determined by the raids. A spirit of solidarity was engendered in the shelters, night after night, and over time people got used to it, and some even chose to take the risk of staying at home.

The poem 'London, September 1940', by **Maurice Lindsay** (131), gives an eloquent account of the early war years in London, at a time when personal relationships were accelerated by the tensions of impending war. Under the 'stuttering bombers' and the searchlights of 1940, the poet remembers attending the ballet with his lover a year ago. But she is lost to him now, in the 'separating fear of distance', and held in someone else's arms. The poem's tensions are balanced by the regular pattern of the rhyme scheme: abab cdcd and a metrical pattern that has each line with four (or sometimes five) strong stresses followed by a line with three strong stresses. The effect is to generate an effective disparity between a sense of cultured calm and order and the 'bewildered terror' of the setting. Lindsay was to become an influential poet, critic and editor in Scottish literary circles after the war, with a similarly balanced lyric style.

Naomi Mitchison gives a vivid picture of London during the Blitz in her poems 'London Burning' and 'Siren Night'. Mitchison moved to her Scottish home in Carradale when war broke out, but she had lived in London for many years and continued to visit the city. Mitchison was well known in literary and political circles throughout the twenties and thirties as a lifelong socialist, a poet, essayist and novelist, and she was one of the first to express concern about the rise of fascism in Germany and totalitarianism in Russia. In these years she wrote a number of major historical novels such as *The Conquered* (1923), *The Corn King and the Spring Queen* (1931), and *The Blood of the Martyrs* (1939), all of which echoed contemporary social and political issues. Thus the persecution of the Christians by the Roman Empire in *The Blood of the Martyrs* made a conscious parallel with the persecution of the Jews in modern Europe.

Her poem 'Siren Night' (152) uses the imagery of ghost stories and fairytales to turn adults into frightened children under the terrors of the Blitz. The edgy, prose-like lines of the poem generate a kind of frantic humour, for no doubt 'Margaret' really was hiding under the piano when the bombs went off, even as 'Tony' pulled the blankets over his head. And we know, too, that 'pale children' really were sleeping in the Underground, except that this is no friendly rabbit burrow in the 'goblin wood', but a reference to the hundreds of citizens who took shelter in the London Tube, sleeping rough on the platforms, night after night. This practice, made famous in drawings by Henry Moore, was initially forbidden but finally had to be accepted by the authorities.

There is a question at the heart of 'Siren Night' that never quite expresses itself, which is 'will there be a happy ending?' In the heat of the moment, the adults revert to denial – 'let us talk about something else', 'let us shut the book', 'let us disbelieve in magic'. And yet there is also a sense of resistance at the end, in the lines 'We set our will against yours, the will of London, / If you kill us, we only die.' This is completely different from the almost hysterical confusion and excitement of the opening lines, and it confirms that these are adults speaking throughout the poem, adults under stress, rather than the voices of actual children. The final effect is all the greater when we come to the nervous understatement, or indeed the hopeful lie, of that last line: 'We are only a little frightened.'

It is typical of Mitchison to acknowledge the genius of Handel, Hayden and Beethoven at a time when anti-German feeling was so rife in Britain, and the reference reminds us of the famous concerts, initiated by the pianist Dame Myra Hess, playing Bach and Beethoven to huddled crowds in the National Gallery (without heating and emptied of its paintings) during the Blitz – even after the Gallery was hit by bombs.

With a more immediately obvious focus on everyday adult concerns, the poem 'London Burning' (150) uses an irregular rhyme scheme and abrupt, colloquial, reported speech to convey the tensions of trying to live from day to day under the Blitz. These tensions appear again with the literary allusions in the poem's closing lines:

> Oh my city, my soul, city of the plain,
> I, like Lot's wife, like Whittington, turn again.

These last references invoke two possible conclusions and two very different fields of meaning. The Bible tells us that Lot's wife was turned to a pillar of salt, for looking back to Sodom and Gomorrah (the sinful 'cities of the plain') as she was led by angels to her salvation, even as God's wrath poured fire on the wicked (Genesis 19). It is not a good ending. The story of Dick Whittington, on the other hand, offers a more positive note, for Dick's decision to return to London ('Turn again, Whittington') leads him to redemption and success. In turning back to 'my city, my soul', during the Blitz, with such echoes in mind, the poet may be accepting either outcome.

Naomi Mitchison is revealingly honest in both these poems when she recognises that, in the face of such danger, death and destruction many people also experienced a terrible intensity and even a forced gaiety that they had never known before. Under cover of the blackout and under the pressure of the times many inhibitions were lost or mislaid. As a writer she was fearless in her approach to taboo subjects and her radical views on female emancipation, sexuality, birth control and abortion in both her essays and her creative writing made her a controversial figure. Her poem 'The Farm Woman: 1942' (153) celebrates the vital contribution made by thousands of women who worked to support the war effort, particularly the 'Land Girls' who laboured in the fields to plant and bring in the crops when so many men were serving in the army. It was hard work and the poem recognises that fact. And yet it also recognises the ambivalences of life during wartime, when the emancipation of women had more than one face, and the disruption of conventional lives and values had more than one outcome.

We can certainly imagine that a woman's hands would be roughened and her body bruised by unaccustomed labour on the farm. But the first three stanzas of this poem seem to be playing with sexual innuendo in a rather disturbing way. First of all, we have to ask 'who is speaking?', because whoever it is seems to be suggesting that the farm woman bears the marks of, at the very least, a romantic encounter. The rhyme scheme repeatedly privileges the (rather suggestive) 'o' sounds of 'show', and 'know', and of course the woman's languid and easy denial. 'Oh no, oh no', as well as the phrase 'And so, and so', sustains the same sound, even as this calm repetition may seem to make her own denial less than fully convincing – 'For I bruise easy'. The oddness of this 'question and answer' structure raises the possibility of a sexual explanation even as the poem seems to deny it. We know that conventional morality was shaken up by the pressures of the war and we have to wonder if that is what is at stake here. Or are we listening to the salacious imagining of some man who cannot deal with a physically competent and independent woman without thinking that such emancipation must have a sexual dimension, too? And perhaps an opportunity for himself? Or is this a fellow Land Girl teasing her co-worker? The ambivalence of the poem is all the stronger for it having been written by a woman. And while the poem seems to hint at some covert sexual experience, these hints do not deny the possibility of the woman's willing pleasure 'in a sweet smother of cries'. On the other hand, the references to bruising and 'too sharp a grip' do not rule out a more violent encounter.

This brilliant little poem seems to invoke both possibilities, and we know that Mitchison's short stories and novels scandalised many readers with their sexual frankness. The poet invokes exactly this unease in ourselves and our culture, and yet at no time does this farm woman seem anything less than a calm and totally self-assured individual. She is no innocent, nor any kind of victim, for this is an adult woman completely at home with both the benefits and the dangers of her own emancipation. Even so, the ambivalence of the poem, and the questions it begins with, remain quietly discomfiting.

The poem ends, however, on a different note and the last two stanzas offer a kind of resolution, for these no longer play with sexual innuendo but make a much clearer statement of intent with a feminist and even a political dimension. Russian women, as seen in newsreels of the time, had claimed their own independence and made the land 'their own' by working on it. The woman in Mitchison's poem is equally strong, for she is fully engaged with the progress of the war, and she works the land despite the sneers of men. Her honour is 'making the crops to grow'. This is an entirely different kind of honour – stronger and more forthright – from the 'honour' or the 'loss' of it that has been hinted at in the earlier verses. Mitchison the feminist and socialist has more than made her point. A later novel by the Scots writer Jessie Kesson used a similar setting, during the second war, to show how the defence of 'national freedom' and the disturbance of the times created different kinds of freedom for women. Kesson's story is a sadder one, however, for the awakening of the young farm wife when she meets an Italian prisoner of war in *Another Time Another Place* (1983) is not achieved without pain.

In her poem 'The Home Fleet' **Olive Fraser** (101) offers a humorous response to the government's commands to 'Dig for

Victory'. She imagines the cabbages in her garden as a fleet of cruisers, named after the cabbage varieties 'Harbinger' and 'Express', just like the cruisers *Ajax* and *Exeter* that had disabled the *Graf Spee* at the Battle of the River Plate in December 1939. Fraser imagines her charges destined for a different kind of plate, however. **Maria Schneider**, who was brought up in Gourock in the years during and after the war, has a more poignant memory of shortages, anxieties and food rationing during her childhood years, when she was asked to draw 'a "live" banana' in her art class – 'Drawing a Banana' (165).

It is appropriate that this section on the 'Home Front' should close with **Flora Garry** and her heartbreakingly quiet poem 'Ambulance Depot, 1942' (107) which speaks, almost in a whisper, of what was at stake in both world wars, and what that meant to the women, wives and families who were left at home to contemplate the true cost of every conflict, then and since. Flora Garry was brought up in Buchan in the North East of Scotland but only started to write poetry in her late thirties after war broke out. Even then, she did not publish a collection of her work until 1974. She is best known for poetry in her native Scots Doric (like her fellow North-Easters Charles Murray, Marion Angus and Violet Jacob) and her work is full of affection for the land, the language and the weather of her homeland. 'Ambulance Depot, 1942' uses English, however, to record another aspect of the kind of work women were recruited to do during the war.

The poem describes an almost domestic scene on Christmas Eve: the depot is still, the war seems to have paused, and the women on stand-by are making a soft toy as a Christmas present for some child. It is 'the hour between tea and black-out', as if 'black-out' was just another gentle routine. The stove is 'snoring', the helmets on the wall have 'little black pot-bellies', a homebound plane overhead has a 'friendly drone', and if anything breaks the silence it is the noisy geese, also going home to their 'sheltering reeds'. There is no phone call alert, and the ambulances 'wait' in the gloom. (A 'purple' alert was a command to extinguish all lighting; a 'red' alert meant that an attack was imminent.) In this quiet suspension the women pass the time making a not very elegant toy duck.

The poet's skill is to create the scene in a succession of simple statements and short sentences in the present tense, telling us what she sees and knows. There are five helmets on the wall and five women at their tasks. The speaker includes herself ('we are making [...] a communal gift') but seems to be a sixth presence, somehow there but not there, uniquely and quietly observant. MacDonald's son may have been killed at sea. Roberts is older and had lost 'someone' in the First World War. She is a little out of place in her new role. Clark and Smith are much younger women, with husbands fighting in North Africa, while Watson's planned engagement has been frustrated by her boyfriend's cancelled leave. Each little history conceals a universe of loss or anxiety, and yet very little is said or shown. Flora Garry's tone is sympathetic but strikingly neutral, and we might consider the effect of this and of her use of surnames only.

The sheltered mood is broken by a few 'eerie' blasts of wind 'assaulting' the hut's 'ramshackle' roof. There's a nervous exclamation or two and the radio is switched on to hear the news that they long for and dread. But it is a hymn that breaks through. 'See, amid the Winter's Snow' is known as a triumphant hymn for Christmas Day, telling of 'peace on earth' and a miraculous child, in the 'cruelly sweet' voice of a boy chorister. The poem ends with four simple and understated lines that, like so much else in this remarkable work, say much more than they seem to. Why is that last line so affecting? What is the difference between saying 'any child', as the poet does, and 'a child'?

THE BURNING WORLD

Strictly speaking the poem 'The Drawings for Guernica' by **Ruthven Todd** (183) refers to an event from the Spanish Civil War, which broke out in 1936 when the deeply conservative rebel forces of nationalism and fascism under General Franco set out to overthrow the left-leaning Spanish Republic. (Some historians would argue that the Second World War actually started here in 1936, or even with the Japanese invasion of Manchuria in 1931.) United in their fear of Communism, Hitler and Mussolini were sympathetic to Franco's cause and the German air force's Condor Legion was called on to bomb the little Basque town of Guernica in the Spring of 1937. This attack is often taken to be the first instance of the bombing of a European civilian population as an act of total war. It caused an international outcry and seemed to confirm the worst fears of what any future war would be like. The event remains an especially potent symbol of these fears because of a famous painting by Picasso, which was done in the same year and exhibited around the world. 'Guernica' is a huge canvas, almost eight metres wide, and Todd's sonnet describes the spirit of the many studies that Picasso made for it. Note how the poet's use of the present tense invokes the moment of time that is always somehow stopped and fixed in any painting – a kind of eternal present – and how that in turn suggests that such suffering is always with us and will never end. This is very true to the impact of Picasso's masterpiece, and certainly those disjointed images of the weeping woman and the frightened child were all too prophetic of what was about to engulf the world in the years to come.

The horrors of that war, and the need to fight it, are invoked again in a chilling poem 'The Traveller' by **Michael Hinton** (129). The poet imagines the speech of a 'traveller', a wanderer, perhaps, who recounts what he saw of the Nazi death camps. He may have been one of the prisoners forced to help, or he may be reflecting on how our frail humanity links us all together – in our compassion and our common guilt: 'We, dear friends, as has often been said, were at the window, / And at the throwing of the switch, and at the burning'. There is a certain formal stiffness to the poem's diction, which is perhaps the only way to convey the horrors it describes. Phrases such as 'Their haste was the less', have the ring of Old English, or even a Gaelic idiom. And indeed the short phrases, heavily punctuated, with an oddly unidiomatic syntax, do seem to be reminiscent of Anglo Saxon verses, with their short stern strongly stressed phrases:

> The <u>cattle</u>-<u>trucks</u> <u>carri</u>ed, <u>sing</u>ing, at the <u>turn</u> of <u>war</u>-<u>tide</u>,
> <u>Jews</u> and <u>Gyps</u>ies, from the <u>battle</u>-<u>fronts</u>, <u>hated</u> <u>people</u>
> <u>Back</u> to <u>unspoken</u> <u>plac</u>es;

The traveller reflects on how this could have been allowed to happen. Either it is 'the casting aside of thought, heed to the blood's voice' or it is a perversion of reason, from those who 'use speech as it is not right to do.' This darkly sober tone, and the closing lines of the poem, do in fact seem to be a conscious echo of the Old English poem 'The Wanderer', in which an old warrior reflects on the impermanence of life, ending 'so spoke the sage in his heart; he sat apart in thought.'[12]

G. S. Fraser (George Sutherland Fraser), only recently graduated from St Andrews, was working as a journalist in Aberdeen when war broke out. Still in his early twenties, poetically inclined and rather bookish by nature, he nevertheless volunteered for military service, and served with the Black Watch for a while before transferring to the Army Service Corps where his skills were put to better use. He spent much of the war working in offices in Cairo and Eritrea, as part of the North African campaign. His early poetry is relatively conventional in formal terms and, although Fraser admired the fire of Hugh MacDiarmid's writing, he chose a more conventional and urbane persona for himself. This voice is very clear in the poems he wrote from the war as if they were 'letters home', rich with nostalgia for happier times. 'A Winter Letter' (98) to his sister is one of these, with its memories of cold autumns in Aberdeen, where he was brought up, and Christmas dances with pretty girls. Fraser uses long conversational unrhymed lines, to dream of Aberdeen as if he and his sister (she is in London) were still walking its frosty streets. The social and domestic details he invokes so tenderly, like his sister's smart clothes, are very far from life in the army, and further still from the heat of 'black Africa', and everything they once knew in peacetime.

A poem such as 'Rostov' (97), on the other hand, gives an unsparing account of the terribly savage tank battles fought on the Eastern front by the river Don in 1941. Like so many of his generation, Fraser had strong socialist sympathies with Russia. (As a student editor, he had published a socialist manifesto in the St Andrews University Magazine only to have the issue suppressed by the university authorities.) The poem's unrhymed long sentences with constantly added clauses 'and ... and ... and', and its rather abstract polysyllabic terms ('the artillery in its tremendous / Asseveration of another existence') generate a sense of impersonal force, like a juggernaut, which is, of course, precisely the point. 'Everything meets its shock' say the guns to the German advance, and under such onslaught 'the thing' begins to 'stagger' just as the German army was forced into retreat that winter. Fraser imagines the shelling as a kind of expression, an 'oratory of the last argument death', saying that 'the wicked / Shall not prosper forever'. The poet imagines the ruthless speeches of Lenin and Churchill as another kind of weapon, and indeed the actual weapons as another kind of speech. Thus Churchill's sentences are like 'the blows of a whip' and Tolstoy and Dostoevsky, whose writings spoke for a creatively renewed Russian spirit in the nineteenth century, are a 'terrible strength'. But if this is a celebration of victory (or at least of German defeat) then the

Scottish War Poetry 1914–1945

language of the poem shows that it was only gained by embracing a ghastly dehumanising force: 'That year it had rained death like apples' (the inappropriately fruitful nature of that image comes as a shock) until everyone involved is indeed part of some 'huge, stupid machine'. A list of such epithets as 'thick', 'numbed', 'broke', 'pawing', 'thundering', 'lumbering' – all in just the first twenty lines – makes the point. The poem closes with a warning about the moment when the *'thing* that you strike / Rouses *itself,* suddenly, very terribly', (my emphasis) to say 'Why do you strike me brother? I am Man.' That shift from inanimate 'thing' to something animate, 'staring with a terribly patient look' – like some animal in the slaughterhouse – is the stuff of nightmare in this inhuman and mechanistic setting.

J. K. Annand's poem 'Arctic Convoy' (91) uses dense Scots and heavily stressed lines to convey a similar sense of the brutal experience of war, in this case the war at sea, on the ships that fought German submarines and the Arctic winter to reach Murmansk and Archangel, bringing supplies to Russia. Note the strong stresses and the alliteration in the following lines, and see how this effect grinds on, thick with consonants, steadily accumulating a relentless weight throughout the length of the poem:

> Northwart, aye northwart, in the pitmirk nicht.
> A nirlin wind comes blawin frae the ice,
> Plays dirdum throu the rails and shrouds and riggin,
> Ruggin at bodies clawin at the life-lines.

Like Annand, the popular Scottish novelist Alastair Maclean served in the navy during these convoys, and this was the setting for his first and perhaps his best book, *HMS Ulysses* (1955). Another classic novel of the Atlantic war, written by a man who commanded frigates on convoy duty, was *The Cruel Sea* (1951) by Nicholas Monsarrat.

In his poem 'S.S. *City of Benares*' (100), **G. S. Fraser** returns to the horrors of total war in writing about the sinking of a passenger ship carrying refugees from Liverpool to Quebec. The steam-ship *City of Benares* included ninety children as part of the nationwide plan to evacuate young people to places of safety, whether from the cities to the countryside, or in this case across the sea to Canada. The convoy was intercepted by a German submarine and the *Benares* was torpedoed and sunk. Seventy-seven of the children were drowned. The news devastated the nation, and something of that shock is conveyed in Fraser's densely compacted and alliterative language, in his tones of almost unbearable ironic rage and despair.

This is clear from the opening lines, and this time the poet has chosen to use insistent rhyming couplets:

> The bell that tolls my syllables can tell
> An underwater tale, clang how there fell
> Suddenly out of a surface shouting world
> Into dumb calm doomed children, and there curled
> (Currents' sick fingers whispering at their hair)
> Round them a coiling clutch, was our despair.

But rhyming couplets usually go with iambic pentameters, or at the very least each line might be expected to match the rhythm of its predecessor. This is not the case here, for Fraser's syntax – the running order of his words and verbs – is convoluted: 'clang how there fell' uses 'clang' as an active verb, though at first reading it seems to play the part of a noun. And 'there fell / 'Suddenly […] into dumb calm doomed children' is a very odd word order. Fraser uses the heaviest alliteration to generate a further kind of stressful reading and the effect can be vividly demonstrated if every alliterative consonant, each pararhyme, and every assonantal vowel is underlined or colour coded in the above passage. Start, for example, with 'bell' 'tolls' 'tell' 'tale' 'fell'. The force of these lines is further compounded by the passage's uneven, but strongly stressed lines, with in some cases, almost every word gaining potential emphasis: 'dúmb cálm doómed chíldren, and thére cúrled' — and look again at the assonance of the vowels and the repeated consonants in '**dUmb / cAlm /dOOm**'.

The end effect of reading such lines aloud is to generate a heavy-footed vocal emphasis that is not idiomatic and certainly not musical, so that it can be difficult to make sense of it. Lines three and four (above) almost need to be decoded before we understand that the syntax is not about 'dumb calm doomed children' but about children who fell out of a 'surface shouting world' into 'dumb calm'. It is also up to the reader to decide whether the 'shouting world' was simply the world of the war and everyday news, or a reference to the screams of the children as the ship went down, to be finally silenced in the 'calm' of the depths.

The image of fingers in a child's hair suggests some sort of caress or maternal care. But here the image is 'sick' for it is the ocean currents at work, and while they too might be curling around the drowning children, in 'a coiling clutch', what the poem actually says is that it is 'our despair' that is 'curled' clutching and 'coiling' around the bodies — just like those sick currents indeed. This is very far from any sort of maternal comfort.

Fraser's extraordinary poem can scarcely contain the 'pressure of horror' that it recreates in these dense, difficult and disturbing lines. The poet's struggle to contain and express his own disturbance is part of what the poem is about, and the lines groan under the fierceness of his demand on us to imagine the horror of the event. The poet's struggle appears again towards the end of the poem, when his ironic rage challenges those of us who would seek comfort in the notion that the little victims are in Heaven now. Mercy is 'deeper than grief', he says, but the betrayal of these children is deeper still. 'Justice is high in heaven', he says, but it is the blood of the innocent that smears the sky, not the flame of guardian angels. The last word of the poem, to devastating effect, is simply: 'unconsoled'.

'S.S. *City of Benares*' must stand for so many other tragic deaths, for the more than fifty million civilians who died during the course of the Second World War. Nor was Fraser alone in understanding this, for another of the finest poems of the war was written by the Gaelic poet George Campbell Hay who tackled the same vision.

Deòrsa Mac Iain Deòrsa / George Campbell Hay, was brought up in Edinburgh but loved to visit Tarbert and the Kintyre peninsula as a boy where he made friends with fishermen, roamed the countryside and fitted-in with the Gaelic speaking community. Tarbert was his father's hometown, but John MacDougall Hay, a minister and novelist mostly remembered as the author of *Gillespie* (1914), died of tuberculosis when his son was only four. George won a Classics scholarship to Oxford and returned to Edinburgh as a teacher. He is one of the very few modern Scottish poets to have written well in all three of Scotland's tongues, and as a gifted linguist he became fluent in European languages too. He was also a committed Scottish nationalist, and when war broke out he refused conscription, like Douglas Young, as a way of challenging the Westminster government's right to conscript Scottish citizens. Young fought his case in court and went to prison for a spell, but Campbell Hay took to the hills and hid out in Argyll for a while before accepting the inevitable and joining the Royal Army Ordinance Corps. He took part in the North African campaign, like so many Scottish soldiers, with later service in Italy and Macedonia. He was sadly marked by his wartime experiences, and once again when he suffered a savage beating in Macedonia in 1946, when Greek fascist nationalists suspected him of communist sympathies because he made friends with local people. The poet was invalided home, suffering a nervous breakdown, and had several relapses and a struggle with alcohol in the post-war years in Edinburgh, until his death in 1984.

Drawing on his Highland roots, and fluent in Gaelic, a language so often ignored or undervalued in official circles at that time, Hay felt a special connection with the common folk of North Africa and Greece, so often despised and exploited to further the colonial ambitions of more developed countries. This sympathy is very marked in his long unfinished poem 'Mochtàr is Dùghall', which imagines a dialogue between two infantrymen, a Highlander and a North African soldier, during the war. They find they have much in common, and indeed Hay had a strong respect for Arab culture. In a letter to Douglas Young he observed that:

> Africa is admirable, and there is a general air of life and a tolerance in small details (probably due to poverty) which are lacking in industrialised N. W. Europe. There is none of the ugliness which is the rule by the Clyde or the Tyne; there is more of natural good manners and less of convention.[13]

It has to be said that many soldiers of the time were quick to despise the native population around them.

In the poem 'Bisearta / Bizerta' (113), the poet finds himself on night guard in 1943, watching the bombardment of the city, flickering silently in the distance. The horror of the moment is all the worse for the silence, yet the poet imagines the 'roar of rage' and the snarls of 'dogs' and the howling of 'wolves' in the eerie beating of those 'wings' of light that seem to scatter and dim the stars themselves. As a strategically vital port in the desert war, occupied by the German and

Italian armies, Bizerta was under attack by the Allied forces. But Hay is not thinking of the soldiers, but of the 'poor streets' and their houses and the screaming of their 'inmates' in an 'amber furnace':

> Is cò a-nochd tha 'g atach
> am Bàs a theachd gu grad 'nan cainntibh uile,
> no a' spàirn measg chlach is shailthean
> air bhàinidh a' gairm air cobhair, is nach cluinnear?
> Cò a-nochd a phàigheas
> seann chìs àbhaisteach na fala cumant?

> (And who tonight are beseeching
> Death to come quickly in all their tongues,
> or are struggling among stones and beams,
> crying in frenzy for help, and are not heard?
> Who tonight is paying
> the old accustomed tax of common blood?)

It is the distance, of course, that ensures the 'ghastly silence' of the bombardment, but Hay's observation that 'you would think' that such a thing would be heard to 'the very edge of the world' implies that such evil *should* be crying out to us all. Instead, that paradoxically beautiful 'ring of rose and gold' continues to flicker in silence and – in the moral sense as well – is heard by no one. The poem intensifies this shame, when the 'light' of the conflagration and the poet's repeated emphasis on its hellish energy ('climbing and sinking', 'reaching and darting', 'declining and leaping in throbs') seem to challenge, in a beautiful last line, the very universe itself.

Hay's Gaelic verses mix a regular syllabic count with recurring rhymes and assonances in the longer lines of each section, but this is not fully reproduced in his own English translation, powerful as it is. 'Esta Selva Selvaggia / This Savage Wood'

(115), on the other hand, is written entirely in English, even if it is densely sprinkled with expressions and curses from French, Italian, Arabic, Greek and German. Hay's linguistic skills, and his classical education allow him to do this, and to cite Dante's *Divine Comedy* in his title, but this is an encounter with the very ugliest face of war.

The *Divine Comedy* begins when the poet Dante feels himself, in his middle age, to be lost in a savage wood, full of rapacious beasts. The poet George Campbell Hay, reluctantly recruited to the war, is in a similarly fearful place, haunted by ever changing voices, events and places that burst on to the page, to be greeted by a barely controlled mixture of fascination, horror and despair. Hay uses drivingly insistent rhymes, irregularly arranged, to reflect on the terrible ironies that face him, here in the cradle of so many civilisations, so familiar from tourist books and art history. But everywhere he looks there is callousness and cruelty, especially in the sudden irruptions of brutal reported speech, as if we were eavesdropping on the violent prejudices and racist talk of battle-hardened soldiers. This, the poem seems to say, is our future and our only common culture: 'sirens, blast, disintegration.' – Tighten your pack straps and march on.

As a lifelong socialist, **Somhairle MacGill-Eain / Sorley MacLean** had longed to serve with the International Brigades against fascism in the Spanish Civil War, but family ties and difficult emotional commitments at the time kept him at home. As a native Gaelic speaker from the Island of Raasay, close to Skye, MacLean, like so many of his generation, remembered being punished for speaking Gaelic in the classroom. He had little cause to love a (Scottish) educational system, and ultimately a government in far-away London, that had so little care for his language and the failing economy of the Highlands. When the time came, however, he was ready to go to war, although his reasons were rather less than conventionally patriotic. He explained his feelings in a letter to Hugh MacDiarmid in 1941:

> My fear and hatred of the Nazis [is] even more than my hatred of the English Empire. [...] The only real war is the class war and I see my own little part merely as one that contributes to the mutual exhaustion of the British and German Empires. I support the British Empire because it is the weakest and therefore not as great a threat to Europe and the rest of the world as a German victory.[14]

MacLean wrote a remarkable sequence of love poems during the 1930s, establishing himself as the finest Gaelic poet of his generation, and indeed the poet who brought Gaelic verse fully into the twentieth century with the power of its contemporary references and its passionately symbolist verses. *Dàin do Eimhir / Poems to Eimhir* (1943) is no conventional love poetry, for its pages mix the pains of love and jealousy with the political anguish of the times, as the poet was haunted by 'all the poverty, anguish and grief / that will come and have come on Europe's people'.[15]

When war broke out MacLean enlisted in the Royal Corps of Signals and was sent to Egypt for the North African Campaign. He was wounded in action twice before being seriously injured by a landmine during the second Battle of El Alamein and invalided home. His war poems from the desert reflect on how he has been uprooted to serve in a global war, far from his homeland. If his Gaelic roots have made him 'a laughing stock' among his fellow soldiers, 'since I was as my people were', ('Dol an Iar / Going Westwards', 134) he is still committed to the fight. Yet despite his hatred of fascism, 'There is no rancour in my heart / against the hardy soldiers of the Enemy, / but the kinship that there is among / men in prison on a tidal rock'. For this socialist poet, too many men are prisoners of systems greater than they are, caught up in imperial and ideological conflicts that are far indeed from their proper home – 'the Island / and every loved image in Scotland.' Even so, 'this is the struggle not to be avoided' and MacLean calls on the warlike traditions of his own culture for strength, 'the big men of Braes [...] the heroic Raasay MacLeods', even as he recognises that the very same culture was no stranger to bloodshed and 'ruinous pride'.

The same compassion for the enemy soldiers, even if they have been recruited to an evil cause, can be found in the poem 'Glac a' Bhàis / Death Valley' (140), where the 'dun sand' in 'a valley gone to seed', so 'dirty yellow and full of the rubbish and fragments of battle' is itself an expression of the tired and grimy futility of war. The dead boy's 'slate grey face' and the flies on the 'grey corpses' make the same point, as if the 'field of slaughter', after the 'delirium' of battle, has been reduced to no more than a ghastly, stale, rubbish dump. Whether this youth was an eager volunteer or an unwilling conscript, there is no meaning, and certainly no pleasure in this shabby end. MacLean's fatigue at the prospect is caught again in the poem's epigraph, which dismisses all the propaganda of glory and leadership in the weary phrase 'some Nazi or other'.

The poet has his own close call with death in 'Latha Foghair/ An Autumn Day' (142) when, after a violent bombardment, he finds himself the only survivor among six dead men. During a long day, under the harshness of the sun, 'so indifferent, / so white and painful', and then 'the stars of Africa, / jewelled and beautiful', sitting on the sand, 'so comfortable, / easy and kindly', he has an existential insight into the meaninglessness of it all. He expresses this by referring to 'Election', which is a concept from his own upbringing in the Free Church, an upbringing he rejected. 'Election' comes from the rigid Calvinist doctrine that insists that some people are predestined to be 'saved' by God's grace and will go to Heaven regardless, while others are forever tainted by original sin, and will be damned, no matter how well they have lived. In the madness of battle, who dies and who lives is another kind of 'election' – the poet lives, and six fellow soldiers sit dead around him, as if 'waiting for a message', simply as a matter of random chance 'without asking us / which was better or worse'.

MacLean's war poems do not invoke the almost unbearable spiritual anguish of George Campbell Hay. There is a resigned calmness to 'An Autumn Day' and 'Death Valley' which are marked by a refusal to dramatise and a refusal to tug at our heartstrings. The poet's own English translations emphasise this, though they miss the fine recurring assonances that are a mark of Gaelic verse. These poems from the Western desert are also different from the guilt and the ideological passion that energised his earlier lyrics in *Dàin do Eimhir*. The war poems were born out of the weariness of actual combat, and a judicious recognition of both the necessity and the futility of war, not to mention the utterly random nature of death and survival. The Gaelic poet never ceased to engage with his own roots, running deep in both pride and shame, but under the desert sun he began to see those roots, and his early enthusiasm for radical revolution, in a different light.

The poem 'Curaidhean / Heroes' (137) is a striking example of this process in action. It opens by recalling the military exploits of three legendary heroes, starting with Marechal Jean Lannes who led Napoleon's troops with much courage in 1809 to capture the town of Ratisbon in Austria. Closer to home, Ruaridh MacLennan fought for the Covenanters against Montrose and the Royalist cause at the Battle of Auldearn in 1645. When all was lost for the Covenanters, MacLennan, a red-bearded warrior six feet tall, refused to give up the standard and was eventually cut down along with his men. Even taller in stature, Gillies MacBain single-handedly attacked a group of English dragoons who were trying to outflank the Jacobite troops at Culloden in 1746. He is said to have dispatched more than a dozen of them before he was slain.

The contrast with an English trooper in Egypt could not be more clear: 'a poor little chap with chubby cheeks / and knees grinding each other.' This is no drinker or brawler, and yet this unattractive little man, with his 'ugly high-pitched voice' was a 'garment of the bravest spirit'. MacLean invokes the horror of the action 'in the smoke and flame / in the shaking and terror of the battlefield' only to subvert it again with an almost laconic delivery:

> Thàinig fios dha san fhrois pheilear
> e bhith gu spreigearra'na dhiùlnach:
> is b' e sin e fhad 's a mhair e,
> ach cha b' fhada fhuair e dh' ùine.
>
> (Word came to him in the bullet shower
> that he should be a hero briskly,
> and he was that while he lasted
> but it wasn't much time he got.)

The oddness of *'should* be a hero' implies some sort of social obligation, rather than pressing military urgency; and the even stranger adjective 'briskly' is equally discomfiting. The next stanza does not hide from the terrible violence of the action, and yet the use of 'biff' to describe a fatal wound, seems very strange and more appropriate, perhaps, to sport or a boxing match. (The Gaelic *deannal* describes a small force, a dash, or a shot as in a turn at something.) This 'hero' will not live in legend, and in fact the poet recognises that the trooper's determination to keep his guns firing has led to the deaths of his fellow artillerymen who had no appetite for fame or medals, nor indeed for death. Note the power of the phrase 'froth from the mouth of the field of slaughter'. Why is that 'froth' so disturbing?

The poem closes with a further reference to Highland history, and perhaps an ironic revision of what that might entail.

Alasdair of Glen Garry was the eleventh chieftain of Clan MacDonald, who fought with the Jacobites at the Battle of Sherrifmuir in 1715. He was widely liked and is largely remembered because the poet Sìleas na Ceapaich, Cicely Macdonald, composed a famous elegy for her chief when he died. The last line of MacLean's poem, echoes the closing lines of Cicely's beautiful lament: 'Alasdair of Glengarry, / you brought tears to my eyes today'. Perhaps Sorley MacLean's poem is a kind of lament, even as it recognises the impossibility of such a formal address among the anonymous and random casualties of mass conscription and modern war.

There may be a further twist to these closing lines, for there is another famous 'Alasdair of Glengarry', who would be Colonel Alastair Ranaldson Macdonell, the fifteenth chief of the Glengarry MacDonalds, best known in a famous portrait by Henry Raeburn in 1812. This Alastair is clad entirely in tartan, wearing his own invention, a 'Glengarry' bonnet, on his head with elaborate dirks and a musket to hand. He is the very picture of a heroic chieftain, who insisted on full Highland dress for himself and his followers. But he was a bad landlord, who felled timber on his land and evicted tenants to make room for sheep farms. His flamboyant concern for appearances and his lack of care for the people of his clan stands for all that is worst in romantic tartanry – far from heroic indeed. If MacLean's poem hints at this figure, too, then his ambivalence about the nature of heroism and the cautious pride he feels for his own descent from 'the big men of Braes' and their 'ruinous pride' is once more called into play.

If that autumn day brought Sorley MacLean to reflect on the random nature of life and death in the desert, then the same setting spoke to **Hamish Henderson** with even more force. After being enlisted with the Pioneer Corps (his eyesight was bad) Henderson was recruited instead by Army Intelligence, where his fluency in French, German and Italian proved to be invaluable. In the North African campaign his task was to interrogate captured enemy soldiers, a job he undertook with skill, compassion and some success. Like MacLean, Henderson's socialist sympathies led him to despise the fascist cause, and yet he, too, can feel no hatred for 'the enemy' as individual soldiers, all thrust into battle (like the Allied troops) by forces larger than themselves. From such insights Henderson came to write his fine long poem sequence *Elegies for the Dead in Cyrenaica* (1948), the single most ambitious poem of the second war. These ten 'Elegies' reflect on the strange nature of the desert campaign, taking place in a harshly hostile and empty space, where soldiers and vehicles on both sides are so covered in dust that it is difficult to tell them apart. Henderson takes this observation as symbolic of a more universal commonality, commenting on 'this odd effect of mirage and looking-glass illusion'[16] as if each side were somehow fighting their own mirror image. This is how he expresses it in 'First Elegy. End of a Campaign' (120):

> There were our own, there were the others.
> Their deaths were like their lives, human and animal.
> There were no gods and precious few heroes.
> What they regretted when they died had nothing to do with
>   race and leader, realm indivisible,
> laboured Augustan speeches or vague imperial heritage.
>   (They saw through that guff before the axe fell.)

More than that, in the existential bareness of the desert, it soon came to seem to Henderson that the final and most important distinction between the two armies was simply the distinction between the living and the dead. And only the dead are truly 'innocent'. All other differences of uniform, creed, motivation or nationality fall away in the face of utter extinction.

Henderson's 'Seventh Elegy. Seven Good Germans' (121) comes directly from his examination of the effects of the dead.

The title echoes the wartime saying that 'the only good German is a dead German', and yet the poem is full of compassion for these ordinary human lives, even for those who 'had trusted in Adolf'. All seven of these soldiers died at El Eleba, a place of no distinction whatsoever, nor did their deaths seem anything other than absurd or accidental. The poem ends with references to the song 'Lili Marlene', a romantic ballad in German about a woman some soldier has left behind. This song became the unofficial anthem of all the troops of the desert war, and despite their leaders' efforts, on both sides, to suppress its popularity, both the 'Desert Rats' and the Afrika Korps took the tune to their hearts. Henderson sees this as another example of human commonality in spite of the propaganda of war, and he ends the poem with the poignant last lines of the song itself: *Wie einst Lili* – 'my own Lili Marlene'.

Hamish Henderson had been brought up in humble circumstances in the Scots speaking communities of Blairgowrie and Glenshee in Perthshire. His mother was a housekeeper who spoke Gaelic so he had an early introduction to both of Scotland's languages and folk culture. Orphaned at thirteen, he was a gifted child and scholarships eventually took him to Dulwich College and a Cambridge education in modern languages. His visits to Germany in the pre-war years cemented his hatred of fascism and confirmed him as a lifelong radical socialist. He was the first to translate into English the writings of Antonio Gramsci, a Marxist theorist who had died in Mussolini's jails in 1937. In the years after the war Henderson took various jobs at home and abroad, but pursued his interest in folk culture and folk music at every opportunity. This enthusiasm was carried over into his own essays, poems and songs, and by the late 1940s he was instrumental in starting a folk-song revival in Scotland. In 1951 Henderson was appointed as a lecturer and researcher in the newly founded School of Scottish Studies at Edinburgh University. For the rest of his life he was a passionate collector of Scots songs and ballads from the oral tradition, and he recorded, supported and gave serious intellectual credit to traditional singers from the travelling folk all round the country.

Henderson's delight in popular expression can be seen in the colloquial verve and the rollicking rhymes of 'Anzio April' (124), and during his wartime service he entertained his fellow soldiers by writing and collecting popular poems and ribald barrack room ballads about everyday army life. His song 'The 51st Highland Division's Farewell to Sicily' (126) refers to the withdrawal of the Highland troops from the Italian campaign, when they were shipped home to take part in the D-Day invasion of Europe. Henderson had been with them in the desert, and during hard times in the taking of Sicily, but he remained behind with the Eighth Army for the next stage of the war, which was to use Sicily as a stepping-stone for the invasion of Italy. The 51st Division had suffered a hard war, even before the desert campaign, for they had been left behind as a rearguard defence during the Dunkirk evacuation in 1940 taking many casualties before they were captured and interned for the duration. After that the Division had to be completely reformed before being sent to North Africa in 1942.

The poem is set to a fine pipe tune from the First World War, 'Farewell to the Creeks', and Henderson said that the words of the poem came to him when he heard it playing on the day, and it was not long before he was singing it to friends in the officer's mess. If the words are linked to the music of this pipe tune the effect is thrilling. Henderson's interest in traditional song and ballad forms is very evident in his use of recurring rhymes and the repetition of phrases and whole lines. Scots terms like 'shaw' (a little wood), 'kyles' (straits), 'bothies' and 'dearie' familiarise an Italian scene, so that it is almost as if the troops are leaving home. The poem makes particularly poignant use of the refrain 'A' the bricht chaulmers are eerie'. This probably refers to the lights of the rooms on the shore, eerie in the gloaming, perhaps, or eerie because the rooms are empty now that the troops have left, but its effect is to suggest a deeper absence –an absence of life and activity, no doubt, but also a melancholy sense of some more permanent loss. The spit and polish and the bravura of the ceremony of shipping out seem all the more moving when we know the hardships the division endured first at Dunkirk, then in North Africa, and those that were awaiting them in Normandy.

The 51st Highland Division features again in the Gaelic poem 'El-Alamein' (145), written by **Calum MacLeòid / Malcolm MacLeod**, where the heat of the desert prompts a longing for home and the cool waters of a favourite well on his native Lewis. Not all the hardships of war have to do with bullets, and a longing for water is also the theme of the poem 'Green, Green is El Aghir' by **Norman Cameron** (96).

Yet another Scottish soldier in North Africa, **Robert Garioch** (Robert Garioch Sutherland was his full name) had been a schoolteacher in Edinburgh when he was conscripted to the Royal Signals Regiment in 1941. He was captured by the Germans during the allied invasion of French North Africa (Operation Torch) in 1942 and interned as a prisoner of war in Italy and then in Germany for the rest of the conflict. Garioch recalled the hardship of those years in his memoir *Two Men and a Blanket* (1975) where the most important things in life came down to the need for a warm blanket and fresh water. He wrote very few poems about the war but 'Property' (102), 'Kriegy Ballad' (103) and 'Letter from Italy' (105) are eloquent accounts of life as a POW. Returned to Scotland, Robert Garioch went on to become a very fine poet in Scots, using the ordinary language of the Edinburgh streets to speak quietly and often satirically on behalf of the common man, forever sceptical of concepts of heroism and the assurances of high command.

Colin McIntyre signed up with the Black Watch, his father's old regiment, and saw service with the Lovat Scouts in Greece in 1946 and with the 6th Airborne Division during the troubles in Palestine. He became one of the 'Oasis' poets during this time, and went on in civilian life to work as a journalist and editor for the BBC. His poems 'Motor Transport Officer' (148) and 'Infantryman' (149) are vividly laconic accounts of actual army experience, similar to Garioch's verses in their grass-roots authenticity, but additionally charged with a striking black humour. The humour and frustration of barrack room life is the subject of 'Gillespie's Leave', by **Jack Gillespie** (111), one of the many verses that he wrote during active service to entertain his fellow squaddies.

J. K. Annand's 'Action Stations' (89) had used a vivid colloquial Scots to catch the everyday language of sailors, from Scotland and England alike, caught up in the heat of action. **Sydney Goodsir Smith** uses Scots to equal effect in his poem sequence *Armageddon in Albyn* (173–7). The poet balances the shorter and starker rhythms of sections I, III and IV ('El Alamein', 'The Convoy' and 'The Sodjer's Sang') against the longer and more musical lines of the other sections ('The Mither's Lament', 'Simmer Lanskip', 'Mars and Venus at Hogmanay' and 'The War in Fife'). 'The Mither's Lament' (174) seems as if it is already traditional, for it is reminiscent of traditional Gaelic laments. Its title and its quatrains (abcb) track Robert's Burn's poem 'The Mother's Lament for the loss of her only son' (abab), which begins 'Fate gave the word, the arrow sped, / And pierc'd my darling's heart'. Smith's poem also echoes lines from the ballad 'Johnny Faa' or 'The Raggle Taggle Gypsies': 'What care I for a goose-feather bed, / With the sheet turned down so bravely, O. / For tonight I'll sleep in a cold open field, / Along with the raggle-taggle gypsies, O'. Less traditional, but certainly in tune with the times, is the mother's repetition of 'doutless', which may actually generate the very doubt she is trying to dispel: 'Doutless he deed for Scotland's life; / Doutless the statesmen dinna lee'. This is a bitter wine, with little mention of 'fate'.

The verses of 'Simmer Lanskip' (176) might have come from a late medieval carol – except for a deliberately discordant ending. A similar shock effect is generated in 'Mars and Venus at Hogmanay' (176) when our expectation of a mood piece with classical references gets a sudden jolt of obscene contemporaneity in the last lines. Yet another perspective is invoked by 'The War in Fife' (177) which calls up the war as only another of the many changes that the little kingdom has suffered, from the decline of fishing to the hardships of mining, in what Smith suggests has been a long history of decline since the Union of the Parliaments surrendered Scottish sovereignty to London.

Born in New Zealand, Sydney Goodsir Smith was brought up in Edinburgh (where his father was a Professor of Forensic Medicine) and went to university at Oxford. He joined the poets and novelists of the modern Scottish Literary Renaissance and adopted Scots as his creative tongue, mixing colloquial speech with the literary Scots of the later medieval Makars. His poetry offers a unique mixture of formal and informal utterance, all the more forceful for the dense music of vowels and consonants that he found and enjoyed so much in his version of Scots.

This is particularly clear in the poem 'October 1941' (178) which invokes one of the hardest years of the war, with the Battle of the Atlantic raging, and the extermination of thousands of Jews in the East, with German troops at the gates of Moscow and the Russian winter drawing on. (G. S. Fraser's poem 'Rostov' dealt with the same sense of crisis.) Goodsir Smith imagines a storm of blood-red leaves swirling across the world – a shuffling, worn-out shroud for 'the wae battalions o the deid'. Nor will there be any respite, for these leaves will still smother the world, even when every tree is bare and 'drained black o tears'. The poem generates an apocalyptic vision of a world at war, where the poet's room, and the trees of an Edinburgh street in a Scottish winter, all seem to be one

Scottish War Poetry 1914–1945

and the same with the mud and the slaughter in Poland and Russia. This is a 'Deevil's Waltz', indeed, rather than the lilting romance of the 'Waltz of Flowers', which is the beautiful last movement of Tchaikovsky's *Nutcracker Suite*.

Smith's dense Scots is an extremely effective medium for this world of tears and leaves, under the storm of a stupid God's breath – 'weirdless', which is to say inept and incompetent. There may be an echo from Shelley's 'Ode to the West Wind' in this poem:

> O wild West Wind, thou breath of Autumn's being,
> Thou, from whose unseen presence the leaves dead
> Are driven, like ghosts from an enchanter fleeing,
>
> Yellow, and black, and pale, and hectic red,
> Pestilence-stricken multitudes: [...]

Smith goes on to use a scattering of assonance, half rhyme, mid-line rhyme, and occasional full rhymes to hint at a mad kind of music in his theme, just as its lines of irregular length keep falling in and out of rhythmic regularity. Each stanza of the poem is composed of only four lines and a repeated refrain, but those lines are very long, they are heavily stressed and dense with alliteration and assonance as they labour together to form each stanza out of only one single sentence. This poem may be the final comment on the madness of war.

REMEMBERING

Hundreds of thousands of men, women and children were caught up in Goodsir Smith's storm of leaves, swirling round a war-torn world; and they were to suffer their own storm of memories in the years to come. **Douglas Young** invokes another torrent in his poem 'For Alasdair' (189), as he finds himself remembering a friend who died in the desert war –

'Haiddan the Germans awa frae the Suez Canal'. Young, a lifelong Scottish nationalist, wonders if this death, like so many others, might not have been on behalf of an imperial agenda that was alien to Scotland's real needs. The poem does not answer the question he asks ('Suld this be Scotland's pride, or shame?') and the only certainty is that his friend is dead. Every bereaved family in the land might have been asking a similar question, along with Goodsir Smith's 'Mither's Lament': was victory worth the loss of my son, husband, father? Back in Scotland, standing fishing by a burn in spate, the poet remembers Alasdair fondly. But even amidst such tender thoughts, the rushing water of the burn has its own comment to make, repeated in the refrain as a disturbed and disturbing force 'whummlan aathing doun', carrying everything away.

Personal loss also invests the poem 'Epitaph' by **William Montgomerie** (158) as he remembers his brother James, a merchant seaman torpedoed on a convoy and drowned in the Mediterranean. The poem is darkly grim, as if his brother's skull 'without a face' were a hollow hourglass with sand in it, tracing the passage of time, now meaningless to him. Nor does time comfort the living, for in the poem 'Thirty Years After' (158) Montgomerie finds himself imagining – or in fact re-living – the trauma of his brother's last minutes. The Montgomerie family belonged to the Plymouth Brethren, a sternly religious Protestant sect. William did not follow his father's faith. Nevertheless, the poem's questioning of divine providence and salvation (or at least a subtle ambivalence about it) bears witness to his pain, even thirty years later.

Alexander Scott served as an officer in the invasion of Europe, fighting in the Ardennes and the Reichswald Forest where he was awarded the Military Cross. He wrote poetry during the war, but chose to publish very few examples of that work in subsequent collections during the years of peace. His poem 'Twa Images' (169) speaks for the trauma of remembrance that afflicted many soldiers on their return to civilian life.

Haunted by memories of the war, and shaken by nightmares of falling to his death among the familiar landmarks of Edinburgh, the poet cannot shake free of these thoughts. The bullet that struck the face of a friend standing next to him, in the last stanza of the second section of the poem, describes an actual incident that happened to Scott. **Robert Garioch** re-lives a similar moment by the seaside in the summer, when a sandcastle and a smoking cigarette end, throws him back to the desert war – 'During a Music Festival' (106). Beethoven's 'Hymn to Joy' from the Ninth Symphony has become a well-loved rallying cry in the celebration of life and brotherhood, but the poem wonders how this can be reconciled with the smoke of war that 'bleeds frae the warld's rim' from the very beginnings of human history.

Edward Boyd served in the RAF, and had a sceptical response to the romance of the 'boys in blue', as his poem 'Visibility Zero' (93) makes clear. As in the case of Colin McIntyre's 'Infantryman', we get a sense that this poem comes straight from the everyday experience of military life. But he, too, remembers his dead in 'Sergeant-Pilot D. A. Crosbie. Coastal Command. Killed in action, 1941' (95), a poem whose laconic lines suggest a silent grief, that plays on the concepts of George Berkley, a philosopher who proposed that 'reality' only exists in the perceptions of the mind, so that if something is not perceived, then it does not exist.

The poem 'ENSA Concert' (94) is also dedicated to a specifically named individual 'In memory of 2nd Lieut. James Peter. Drowned, Dunkirk, 1940'. It is as if Boyd is making a conscious effort to memorialise these losses in long titles like this, honouring his dead friends with a precise account of their names and the circumstances of their demise. 'ENSA' stands for the 'Entertainments National Service Association', an organisation set up to boost the morale of troops with concerts and shows at home and abroad. Popular music often has the power to throw up past memories and this poem is an almost unbearably poignant example of that, as the poet experiences a flashback to happier times by the seaside with James. This is certainly a poem about memory, but its lines go on to link that 'golden day' in the past, watching the gulls dive at the beach, with the chaos of Dunkirk and the plunging bombers. So both past and present co-exist: 'once again the sand / is filtering through our fingers / and with it goes our youth'. In addressing the past as if it were present – 'Did you remember that golden day, / the day war swallowed us up' – the poet understands that he, like his dead friend, has not really escaped, but has in fact been 'swallowed up' as well. This poem in its modest way, and in this most personal cry, speaks for all the best poetry of the Second World War, and for all those who were engulfed by it. Boyd lived to have a successful career as an author and screenwriter in later years, known for radio plays, and for his work on the TV series *Z Cars* and *The View from Daniel Pike.*

Edwin Muir was in his fifties, living in St Andrews and working as a critic and reviewer when war broke out. His engagement with the modern world was hugely influenced by an idyllic childhood on his father's croft on Wyre, a remote island in the Orkneys, where he experienced a simple quality of life that had not changed much since the eighteenth century. His memories of his own golden days were all the more profound when the family moved to the industrial horror that was Glasgow in 1901. Muir, then in his teens, suffered the death of both his parents and two of his brothers within four years of arriving in the city. He did not much like the modern world, and in the coming years his poetry was to be haunted by images of a mythic timelessness and a lost Eden. As a poet he looked for the 'fable' – the essential and timeless truth – that somehow lies beneath the details of each everyday 'story'. This is the creative vision that prompted his poem 'The River' (164), which sees time as a stream that somehow reflects war as an endless recurrence, travelling across the world, so that at different times in the poem we are not sure whether he is describing the marching troops of the 1940s, or the legions of Rome. An old woman clasps her grandson's shoulder, but he is 'Bristling with spikes and spits and bolts of steel, / Bound in with belts' and is already distant from her, already standing in a 'new world'.

This is a world of broken links and destruction: 'a blackened field, a burning wood, / A bridge that stops half-way' and as the poem's steady, unrhymed, descriptive sentences unfold we realise that it could be describing the bombing of London and Berlin, or the destruction of Carthage; or rather it is describing both events and thousands like them throughout human history. The destruction is all the more strange and inescapable because the poem makes it seem as if it is all happening by itself:

> Pillars and towers and fans and gathered sheaves
> Hold harvest-home and Judgment Day of fire.
> The houses stir and pluck their roofs and walls
> Apart as if in play and fling their stones
> Against the sky to make a common arc
> And fall again.

Here 'harvest home', a celebration of fertility and bounty has been collapsed into 'Judgement Day', the final reckoning of all our sins – a terrible harvest indeed. The power and the poignancy of Muir's poem is bound up with a timeless perspective, which is made to seem almost inevitable, as if entirely free of human will or intervention. Is that the case? Is war an inescapable part of the human condition?

> The stream
> Runs on into the day of time and Europe,
> Past the familiar walls and friendly roads,
> Now thronged with dumb migrations, gods and altars

> That travel towards no destination. Then
> The disciplined soldiers come to conquer nothing,
> March upon emptiness and do not know
> Why all is dead and life has hidden itself.
> The enormous winding frontier walls fall down,
> Leaving anonymous stone and vacant grass.
> The stream flows on into what land, what peace,
> Far past the other side of the burning world?

Perhaps the question that Muir asks in those closing lines, with the pointless futility he sees there and yet, perhaps, the hope of a distant peace, make 'The River' the most appropriate poem to conclude this study of the poetry of war, its compassion, its courage, its pain, and the terrible questions it raises.

NOTES

1 'The Unspoken', Edwin Morgan, *Collected Poems* (Manchester: Carcanet Press, 1990), p. 182.
2 First published in *Poems of Wilfred Owen*, ed. by Edmund Blunden (London: Chatto & Windus, 1933).
3 Philip Larkin, 'MCMXIV', in *The Whitsun Weddings* (London: Faber & Faber, 1964), p. 28.
4 '1914 I. Peace', *The Poetical Works of Rupert Brooke*, ed. by Geoffrey Keynes (London: Faber & Faber, 1960), p. 19. The sonnet sequence ends with 'V. The Soldier', which is discussed later in this book.
5 A. D. Gillespie, *Letters from Flanders* (London: Smith, Elder, 1916), p. 313.
6 Carl Von Clausewitz, *On War* [1832–35], ed. by Beatrice Heuser (Oxford: Oxford University Press, 2008).
7 Sigmund Freud, 'Beyond the Pleasure Principle' [1920], in *The Standard Edition of the Complete Psychological Works of Sigmund Freud*, vol. 18, ed. by James Strachey (London: Hogarth Press, 1955).
8 Samuel Hynes, *A War Imagined: The First World War & English Culture* (London: Bodley Head, 1990), p. x.
9 Cecil Day Lewis, 'Where are the war poets?' in *The Complete Poems*, (Redwood City CA: Stanford University Press, 1992), p. 335.
10 Naomi Mitchison, *You May Well Ask: a Memoir, 1920–1940* (London: Victor Gollancz, 1979), p. 222.
11 'Interview: The many realities of Edwin Morgan', Judith Palmer, *The Independent*, 25 November 1997.
12 'The Wanderer', trans. Michael Alexander, *The Earliest English Poems* (Harmondsworth: Penguin Classics, 1966), p. 73.
13 George Campbell Hay, *Collected Poems and Songs of George Campbell Hay*, ed. by Michel Byrne, vol. II (Edinburgh: Edinburgh University Press, 2000), p. 32.
14 To Hugh MacDiarmid, 8 March, 1941, quoted by Joy Hendry, 'Sorley MacLean: the Man and his Work', in Raymond J. Ross and Joy Hendry (eds.), *Sorley MacLean: Critical Essays* (Edinburgh: Scottish Academic Press, 1986), p. 27.

15 'The Cry of Europe' in Sorley MacLean, *From Wood to Ridge, Collected Poems in Gaelic and English* (Manchester: Carcanet, 1989), p. 9.
16 Foreword to the 1948 edition of *Elegies for the Dead of Cyrenaica* (Edinburgh: EUSPB, 1977), p. 59.

SELECT BIBLIOGRAPHY

Critical and Contextual Studies
Angus Calder, *The People's War: Britain 1939–1945* (London: Pimlico, 2008)
Carl Von Clausewitz, *On War* [1832–35], ed. by Beatrice Heuser (Oxford: Oxford University Press, 2008)
Santanu Das (ed.), *The Cambridge Companion to the Poetry of the First World War* (Cambridge: Cambridge University Press, 2013)
Simon Featherstone, *War Poetry: An Introductory Reader* (London: Routledge, 1995)
Sigmund Freud, *Beyond the Pleasure Principle* [1920], in *The Standard Edition of the Complete Psychological Works of Sigmund Freud*, vol. 18, ed. by James Strachey (London: Hogarth Press, 1955)
Paul Fussell, *The Great War and Modern Memory* (Oxford: Oxford University Press, 1977)
Paul Fussell, *Wartime. Understanding and Behaviour in the Second World War* (Oxford: Oxford University Press, 1989)
Juliet Gardiner, *Wartime: Britain 1939–1945* (London: Headline, 2004)
Adrian Gregory, *The Last Great War: British Society and the First World War* (Cambridge: Cambridge University Press, 2008)
Samuel Hynes, *A War Imagined: The First World War and English Culture* (London: Bodley Head, 1990)
Tim Kendall (ed.), *The Oxford Handbook of British and Irish War Poetry* (Oxford: Oxford University Press, 2007)
Richard Overy, *The Bombing War: Europe 1939–1945* (London: Penguin Books, 2014)
Adam Piette, *Imagination at War: British Fiction and Poetry, 1939–1945* (London: Papermac, 1995)

Adam Piette and Mark Rawlinson (eds), *The Edinburgh Companion to Twentieth-Century British And American War Literature* (Edinburgh: Edinburgh University Press, 2012)

Trevor Royle (ed.), *In Flanders Fields: Scottish Poetry and Prose of the First World War* (Edinburgh: Mainstream, 1990)

Trevor Royle, *The Flowers of the Forest: Scotland and the First World War* (Edinburgh: Birlinn, 2006)

Trevor Royle (ed.), *Isn't all this Bloody?: Scottish Writing from the First World War* (Edinburgh: Birlinn, 2014)

Trevor Royle, *A Time of Tyrants: Scotland and the Second World War* (Edinburgh: Birlinn, 2013)

Randall Stevenson, *Literature and the Great War 1914–1918* (Oxford: Oxford University Press, 2013)

Hew Strachan, *The First World War* (London: Simon and Schuster, 2003)

Jay Winter, *Sites of Memory, Sites of Mourning: The Great War in European Cultural History* (Cambridge: Cambridge University Press, 1996)

FURTHER READING

FIRST WORLD WAR
Fiction
   Pat Barker, *The Regeneration Trilogy* (*Regeneration;
      The Eye in the Door; The Ghost Road*) (1991–1995)
   Sebastian Faulks, *Birdsong* (1993)
   Lewis Grassic Gibbon, *Sunset Song* (1932)
   Erich Maria Remarque, *All Quiet on the Western Front*
      (1929)

Memoir
   Edmund Blunden, *Undertones of War* (1928)
   Vera Brittain, *Testament of Youth* (1933)
   Robert Graves, *Goodbye to All That* (1929)
   Siegfried Sassoon, *Memoirs of an Infantry Officer* (1930)
   Ernst Jünger, *Storm of Steel* (1920)

SECOND WORLD WAR
Fiction
   Eric Linklater, *Private Angelo* (1946)
   Alistair Maclean, *HMS Ulysses* (1955)
   Nicholas Monsarrat, *The Cruel Sea* (1951)
   Geoffrey Wagner, *The Sands of Valour* (1967)
   Joseph Heller, *Catch–22* (1961)

Memoir
   Stephen Ambrose, *Band of Brothers* (1992)
   Anne Frank, *The Diary of a Young Girl* (1947)
   Martha Gellhorn, *The Face of War* (1959)
   Art Speigelman, *The Complete Maus* (2003)
   Daniel Swift, *Bomber County* (2010)

Lightning Source UK Ltd.
Milton Keynes UK
UKHW020219151218
334042UK00005B/362/P